ENDORSEMENTS FOR *BECOMING CHINESE*

As a second-generation Chinese American through my father and a third-generation Chinese American through my mother, I found Rev. Dr. Ng's book deeply reflective of the Asian American experience, capturing our journey from shame to pride and from uncertainty to full self-acceptance.

—Rev. Kathryn Choy-Wong, Inter-cultural Consultant, author of *Building Lasting Bridges*

Lauren Lisa Ng writes with factual detail and emotional depth, blending familial intimacy with historical breadth through self-reflection and others' perspectives. She explores the yin and yang of her body and story. I alternately chuckled and recoiled, and I couldn't put it down.

—Rev. Dr. Sharon T. Koh, Executive Director/CEO, International Ministries

In *Becoming Chinese*, Lauren Ng traces her growth as a Chinese American amid rising anti-Asian hate. Revisiting her hybrid upbringing, she reveals the roots of her advocacy and ministry, writing with bodily imagery that ultimately speaks from the heart and moves the reader.

—Russell Jeung, PhD, Professor, Asian American Studies, Co-Founder, Stop AAPI Hate

Becoming by remembering. Ng reflects, weaves, and names seemingly disjointed experiences to reveal their connections. This anthology presents an embodied, integrated identity and offers a powerful companion for readers seeking awakening without living divided lives.

—Raymond Chang, President, Asian American Christian Collaborative (AACC) / Executive, TENx10, Fuller Seminary

Spanning scalp to soles, *Becoming Chinese* showcases Lauren Lisa Ng's poetic dexterity. Her searing yet graceful essays invite readers to taste and see sacred beauty amid bitterness and sweetness, leaving stories that linger beyond the final page, ready to be savored again.

—Rev. Dr. Jamie Washam, Senior Minister of the
First Baptist Church in America

Becoming Chinese by Lauren Lisa Ng is a luminous and courageous essay collection tracing a lifelong journey of cultural becoming. With honesty and grace, Ng explores identity, family, faith, and Asian American experience, offering a resonant mirror for anyone who has lived between worlds.

—Rev. Chakravarthy Zadda MSc, PhD, Senior Pastor,
First Baptist Church of Waukesha, Wisconsin

As a fellow minister and public servant, I find Ng's reflections on faith, ancestral strength, and hard-won self-reclamation a vital balm for diverse communities. This timely memoir offers a luminous guide for embracing identity and navigating the river of cultural belonging.

—Aidsand F. Wright-Riggins, Executive Director Emeritus,
American Baptist Home Mission Societies and
Mayor of Collegeville, Pennsylvania

In *Becoming Chinese*, Lauren Lisa Ng offers a courageous, deeply personal exploration of culture, faith, and identity. Her thoughtful, disarming essays express lived theology and invite reflection on belonging and self-discovery, revealing why she is one of my heroes.

—Rev. Thomas L. Bowen, General Secretary,
Progressive National Baptist Convention

BECOMING CHINESE

Essays on Self-Discovery from Head to Toe

Lauren Lisa Ng

Becoming Chinese: Essays on Self-Discovery from Head to Toe

Published by Inspirit Judson Press, Valley Forge, PA 19482-0851

Interior design by Crystal Devine.
Cover design by Gregory Ng.

Cataloging-in-Publication Data available upon request.
Contact cip@judsonpress.com.

Printed in the U.S.A.

First printing, 2026.

For my parents, who gave and gave,
and still give

CONTENTS

ix Preface

1 Hair

8 Eyes

20 Ears

30 Nose

38 Mouth

47 Belly

56 Hands

64 Legs

74 Feet

PREFACE

As an Asian American woman in the post-COVID world, I became inspired to write these essays after reading Korean American author Michelle Zauner's *Crying in H Mart*. Zauner's memoir—set against the landscape of her mother's cancer diagnosis—was relatable to thousands of Asian women in particular, due to its focus on food as a cultural center, familial relationships and expectations, and the pain and beauty of self-discovery.

I've read dozens of books like Zauner's, always with great enjoyment. It is a special thing to see oneself on the published page, to recognize the sights, sounds, and smells of such colorful and thick descriptions of people and places. I found myself reading aloud to my spouse (who is neither Asian nor a woman) full sections of *Crying in H Mart*, desperate for him to share in my marvel over how much it mirrored my own life experience: *Listen to this, honey! My mom does the same exact thing!*

And yet, the paths I share with writers like Zauner eventually get narrower and narrower until they abruptly end on the river's edge that separates me as a second-generation American from those who are closer to the immigrant experience. Those writers have memories of parents teaching them their first words in their mother tongues. They benefit from grasping languages, spoken and unspoken, that allow them to order food in a restaurant or interpret the nuance in a seemingly unweighted gesture. They take regular trips back to the countries of their birth to visit cousins, aunts, and uncles who eagerly anticipate their return. Those writers stand on the other side of that wide river, waving to me across the strong current. I see them, but I cannot cross.

Both sets of my grandparents immigrated to the United States. My mother did, too, from Singapore when she was eight. My father was born in Boston. I was born in 1978 and raised in a middle-class suburb of Chester County, Pennsylvania, about thirty minutes west of Philadelphia. English was my first and only language. My formative years were the 1980s and '90s, and I enjoyed a steady diet of television from *Sesame Street* and *Mister Rogers* to *The Brady Bunch* to *Growing Pains* and *Beverly Hills 90210*. I made mixtapes, clipped my mustard yellow Sony Walkman to my belt like a prize, and dreamt of being Debbie Gibson's saxophonist when I grew up. I had magazine subscriptions to *YM* and *Seventeen*. I played soccer, field hockey, and lacrosse, sang in church and school choir, and went to Rita's Water Ice with my friends on the weekend. In high school I became class president, editor of the yearbook, and was voted onto homecoming court two years in a row. I didn't know a single word of Chinese (Cantonese or Mandarin) and had never traveled to China. Besides my big brother, Greg, I had zero Chinese friends.

Therefore, this book is decidedly Asian American in its perspective and timbre. I was born Chinese, but it has taken me forty-seven years and counting to become Chinese. You might call this recent revelation of mine an act of reclaiming my culture. You might call it maturation, a simple settling into one's skin that tends to happen around the mid-life mark. You might call it a celebration of self, made possible by recent shifts in the American ethos that has dislocated its historic center to allow for more and more voices to be heard. Whatever it is, I suspect—hope, even—that there are others like me who were born something but still find themselves in the act of becoming that very thing. I hope my ponderings will provide more mirrors for them to look upon and possibly see themselves. I hope there will be others on the same side of the river as me.

HAIR

The Raggedy Ann book I kept within nightly reach as a child captivated me. I was around eight years old when it became part of my bedtime routine to page through it, cover to cover. The plot of the book was that all the toys in the playroom came alive at night—a trope that in the 1980s had not yet been made popular by the *Toy Story* franchise. I was especially enchanted by a collection of dolls who were on one page lifeless, their limbs bent at almost grisly angles, and then became, on the next page, animated into living, talking companions: a lonely child's dream.

I was never drawn to Raggedy Ann herself. I found her haunting with her head of yarn, beady, black eyes, and triangular nose. It was another doll that compelled me to open the book night after night. This doll's skin was the color of ivory, and she had a perfect pink circle brushed onto each cheek. Her hair didn't look like yarn but like silk. It was yellow as sun-soaked corn, pulled up into pigtails with tight ringlets that fell to her shoulders. That doll was the only one I wished would come alive for me, the reader. I wanted that blonde-haired doll in a way I had never wanted anything before. It's fair to say I yearned for her. I imagined that if she could leap off the page as a living and breathing creature, she would sit cross-legged on the other side of my four-poster bed, and we'd stay up late whispering and giggling while she taught me how to curl my hair just like hers. I would ask her to teach me how to be beautiful and how to get the blonde girls at school to like me. She would go with me everywhere, and through her companionship, I would gain acceptance and approval by others.

Eventually, my fascination with golden hair shifted to real kids. Sandy Satinsky was one of the tallest girls in my class with hair so flaxen it was almost white. I would stare at Sandy's hair during class, in awe of how effortlessly it fell to her shoulders, cut bluntly to a perfect edge that somehow remained straight, even when she moved her head from side to side. My breath would catch in my throat whenever Sandy ran her fingers through those silvery strands, tossing it almost entirely to one side so that the part was over her ear. As she let go with her hand, Sandy's hair would cascade back into place like clear waves upon a beach.

You can imagine my excitement when both Sandy and I received invitations to a birthday sleepover for another girl in our class named Katie. The night of the party, we all finished our pizza and cake and headed to the basement where microwave popcorn was distributed in bowls and *Nightmare on Elm Street* was queued up on the VCR. We spread out our sleeping bags and got ready to change into our pajamas. I pulled my nightshirt from my duffel bag and turned away from the other girls for some privacy. As I bent slightly over to slide my arms out of my top, I suddenly felt a cold rush of wind on my bottom half. I frantically pulled at my pants that had been yanked down to my ankles, but my hands were caught inside my sleeves like fingers in a Chinese finger trap.

Amidst my desperation and confusion, I could hear Sandy shrieking excitedly. When I finally managed to free my head and arms, I looked to see her doubled over, her azure eyes glossy with tearful laughter. She looked proud of her clever prank. Katie and the other girls were giggling too, but in that uncomfortable way kids do at that age, with relief that it had happened to someone else instead of them. By the time I managed to pull up my pants, the girls had become preoccupied with something else. I ran upstairs to find the bathroom where I sat on the edge of the cornflower blue bathtub for several minutes, slowly recomposing myself. I had been singled out and both the subtle and obvious differences I'd been calculating between me and those other girls finally felt official. When I managed to leave the bathroom, I asked Katie's parents if I could use their phone to call my mom who promptly came to pick me up.

In the period between March 13 and September 15, 2020, Donald J. Trump used the following expressions a total of 319 times in public, via speeches from his election campaign or rallies, talks at presidential events or meetings, interviews and press conferences, or tweets or re-tweets on the platform formerly known as Twitter: *China flu*, *China plague*, *China virus*, *Chinese plague*, *Chinese flu*, *Chinese virus*, *Wuhan virus*, and *Kung flu*.[1] The effect his rhetoric has had on the American public consciousness is still being examined by a wide array of researchers.

My data set comes from personal experience. At the onset of the pandemic, in those first months when we were still standing outside on our decks every evening at 7:00 pm whooping and hollering for first responders, when we were wiping down each item from the grocery store with sanitizing wipes, when we were hand painting river rocks with motivational messages to leave around the neighborhood, I donned two layers of facial masks everywhere I went. With most of my face covered, I would stand uncomfortably in line at the pharmacy or anxiously bag my food at the end of the conveyor belt, eager to get in and out of any establishment as quickly as I could. It wasn't just the threat of the coronavirus that made me want to skedaddle; it was the concern that the anti-Asian rhetoric being spewed by our president would have real-life consequences for me in my little suburban neighborhood in northern California.

I remember walking out of the pharmacy one morning in the early days of the shutdown. Two men were standing next to a pickup truck in the parking lot, conversing. They looked up at me, glanced away, and then did a double take, eventually tracking me all the way to my car with their stares. My mask covered most of my face, and I was too far away for them to see the curvature of my eyes, so I knew it was my long, black hair that gave me away. The men tracked me overtly and with intention, even shifting their bodies so they could remain focused on me as I hurried to my car, crawled inside, locked the doors, and drove away.

I wonder if having a towheaded companion would have made a difference for me in that moment, or for the thousands of Asians in the United States who have reported hate incidents since the pandemic began. I know when kindhearted people in communities around the country began to volunteer to walk with Asians—specifically Asian elders—as they ran errands or went for their daily exercise, it granted our Asian community some comfort. Surely, the risk of someone approaching us with nefarious intent would severely diminish with a white man or woman by our side! There is some physical and ideological safety that comes by being adjacent to the dominant culture's notion of the ideal. But safety through adjacency will only last for so long. People can betray you to stay in the good graces of those who might pose a threat. Walking companions may get you to your front door, but then they must return to their lives. And no one can protect you from harm just by having stood beside you while the harming occurred. Adjacency is a borrowed and short-lived safety.

My hair has gained me unsolicited attention in my work, too. In my early twenties I was enrolled at the American Baptist Seminary of the West in Berkeley, California, on track to earn my Master of Divinity degree. I'd discerned a call to ministry and knew I wanted to devote my life to serving others. In my second year of the three-year academic program, I was assigned as a Minister-In-Training at a church in Oakland.

It was a crisp autumn Sunday morning when I woke up before my alarm after a restless night of sleep. I was anxious because this was the day I'd preach my very first sermon in front of a congregation. I pulled on my blouse, slacks, and heels and headed to the church. Sitting in the robing room before the service began, I read over my manuscript once more, zipped up my clerical robe, smoothed my hair, and said a prayer.

The worship service was beautiful. And while I knew I had a number of things to work on to improve my homiletical approach, I was feeling good about how it all went. After the organ postlude, everyone moved into the fellowship hall for coffee hour. There I was, sipping my lemonade, when one of the congregants approached me.

"That was a wonderful sermon," said the older gentleman as he came to stand beside me.

"Thank you so much," I replied with a soft smile.

"Good treatment of the biblical text. And you also projected your voice very well." He took a sip of his coffee. "The only critique I'd offer is to tie your hair up when you preach. You'll look more professional and appropriate behind the pulpit that way. Wearing it down is a distraction to those of us in the pews."

I breathed in sharply, not sure at first that I'd heard him correctly. But as his words began to take root, I managed a simple reply: "Thank you for the feedback."

I had never thought of my hair as a distraction to others, much less as something that might get in the way of a worshipper being able to focus on God and Christ's teachings. My hair, when worn down and long, is a symbol of longevity and prosperity in my Chinese culture. Also, I sometimes just like it that way, depending on my mood or my outfit. And yet it seems that many find my hair to be problematic, distracting, inappropriate, foreign, threatening even. I wonder if that older gentleman at the church would have offered such a critique to a woman with blonde, brown, or red hair. Would he have offered it to a white woman? Might the centuries-old objectification and hyper-sexualization of Asian women in the white male gaze have had anything to do with him being so distracted by my long black hair?

More than twenty years later, I think of this man whenever I get ready to preach. My hair is still mostly black but now features strands of silver interwoven like a piece of *Gintsugi* pottery. The broken parts mended. The scattered pieces joined back together. Healing and a new kind of wholeness on full display.

On April 15, 2022, I got my first tattoo. It was Good Friday, and I was at lunch with a close friend of mine. She and I had talked for years about getting tattoos, so much that it had become a joke every time we went out together. "Ready for that tattoo?" I'd ask, and she would smile, pretend to ponder the thought, and then say, "Hmm, tempting. . . ." On this sunny afternoon, we had plans to grab Vietnamese food and walk around town a bit. We didn't have long, as we both had Good Friday services to attend that evening. While we enjoyed our vermicelli bowls, I asked my typical question. This time my friend replied, "Hmm, maybe!"

A couple hours later, we were in the tattoo parlor we had found with a quick Google search, waiting to get inked. My friend had had her design picked out for years. I had ideas but nothing had risen to the top of my heavily populated "Tats" Pinterest board. As I sat in the waiting room, the buzzing sounds of tattoo guns and giddy customers filling the air, I opened Pinterest and began to scroll through my collected images. I had recently been gathering images of Chinese combs and hairpins decorated in green and white jade, pearls, gemstones, and seashell. I stopped on the last one—an illustration of an ancient Chinese comb featuring three swallows soaring amid clouds made of jade and attached by a gold bail atop elegant tines of tortoise shell.

Hairpins and combs are often family heirlooms that date back centuries in Chinese culture. They are considered tokens of love. A Chinese woman might give one to her fiancé in the days leading up to their wedding, after which the husband returns it to his new wife by placing it in her hair. Sometimes these adornments were broken in half by lovers forced to be apart for some time; they would each hold on to their half with the hope of one day being reunited.

But the tradition that speaks to me most is when a Chinese comb is used by a mother to brush her soon-to-be-wed daughter's hair on the eve of the matrimonial ceremony. A silent, tender ritual of bringing near what is about to become distant, of combing through years of memory so the daughter will never forget, of leaving her with something she can always take with her. A proximate symbol of belonging, of security, of safety. That afternoon in the tattoo parlor, the image of this jade and tortoise shell comb captured my spirit and was soon permanently inked onto my left arm. Every time I see it, I am reminded of the ancient Chinese custom in which a blessing for happiness, harmony, and longevity is recited by a mother, as the comb is pulled through her daughter's raven hair once, twice, a third time, and then a fourth, from the crown of her head down to the wavering edge, like calm black waters lapping under the dark of night.

NOTE

1. Robin Kurilla, "'Kung Flu'—The Dynamics of Fear, Popular Culture, and Authenticity in the Anatomy of Populist Communication," Frontiers in Communication 6 (2021): 624643. doi: 10.3389.

EYES

I hadn't been this excited to see a movie in the theater since November 1984 when Helen Slater brought Supergirl to the big screen in her red cape and boots. My mom took me to see that film, and I remember giddily absorbing every minute of Kara Zor-El's mission to retrieve the glowing Omegahedron from outer space, and eventually from the clutches of the villainous witch, Selena, all while managing lovesick Ethan who had fallen for her at first sight after drinking a magic potion. Here was my favorite superhero, whose action figure I played with every day, alive and majestic right before my eyes. The movie failed horribly at the box office, but I didn't care. I was six years old and completely under its spell.

Now, at age forty, I was the mother taking her kids to the movies. I clutched my twelve- and ten-year-old daughters by the hand and led them to our seats in the darkened theater. We settled into our "luxury loungers"—the plush, reclining seats our local cinema advertises as its main selling point—plunked our ICEEs into our cup holders, distributed buttery popcorn evenly among the three of us, and looked around. As Maria Menounos hosted her Noovie trivia games on the screen above us, streams of Asians were pouring into the theater. I couldn't believe my eyes. *Who were all these people and where have they been hiding?* My predominantly white neighborhood in northern California had surely never seen this high a concentration of Asians in its theater before. I nudged my daughters and nodded toward a family sliding into the row behind us. "Look, girls! A whole Asian family!"

"Mommmmmm!" they pleaded, their eyes desperate with humiliation. "Okay, we *see*! Please stop!" whispered my eldest daughter.

The lights dimmed some more. I grasped my daughters' hands again, squeezed, and said, "Girls, I just want you to understand how big a deal this is. For your mommy, this is like a dream come true." The production logos began to roll, the sound of a woman singing a lounge tune in Chinese filled the air, and a quote by Napoleon Bonaparte appeared in white font against a black background: *Let China sleep, for when she wakes, she will shake the world.* My eyes widened and my heart quickened. I was under a new spell.

Crazy Rich Asians would go on to earn $239 million worldwide, making it the highest-grossing romantic comedy of the 2010s. Directed by John M. Chu and based on the novel by Kevin Kwan, the movie earned several nominations and awards for its vibrant, extravagant tale of Asian American New Yorker Rachel Chu (played by Constance Wu). Rachel accompanies her boyfriend, Nick (played by Henry Golding), to a wedding in Singapore while completely unaware that Nick hails from an extremely wealthy Singaporean family and is considered one of that country's most eligible bachelors. The release of *Crazy Rich Asians* was a watershed moment for the representation of Asian Americans, not just in cinema but also in popular American culture.

I can count on my two hands the number of Asians I was exposed to on both the big and small screens growing up. There was Short Round in *Indiana Jones and the Temple of Doom* (1984), played by Ke Huy Quan, who also portrayed the character Data in *The Goonies* (1985). There was Long Duk Dong, played by actor Gedde Watanabe, in the 1984 coming-of-age comedy, *Sixteen Candles*. I remember watching that Molly Ringwald movie with friends in high school.

Watanabe would enter a scene, announced by the sound of a crashing gong, and shout, "Whass happenin', haaht stuff?" Each time he said this, I wanted to crawl under a rock in shame as if Long Duk Dong were my first cousin and I were somehow responsible for interpreting his awkward, embarrassing behavior to my friends. I couldn't explain then what I can explain now: that with so few Asians portrayed in popular culture at that time, each one became a reductive representation of who we were in the dominant American psyche, as well as an unwitting repository for all the hopes, disappointments, and characterizations of our diverse AAPI communities as we struggled for visibility and acceptance in that same psyche.

There were some more positive portrayals. In 1986, Tamlyn Tomita starred with Ralph Macchio and Pat Morita in *Karate Kid II*, and I was awestruck by this beautiful, young Asian girl playing the love interest of heartthrob Daniel LaRusso. In 1994, comedian Margaret Cho landed a sitcom called *All-American Girl*, and I marveled at the possibility that this Asian American family could be just like the Seavers, the Keatons, or the Huxtables. Unfortunately, *All-American Girl* only lasted for one season.

In my freshman year of high school, my history class read *The Good Earth* by Pearl S. Buck and then watched the 1937 film adaptation. The only Asian kid in class, I sank into my seat as white actors Luise Rainer and Paul Muni donned yellowface for their portrayals of Chinese farmers O-Lan and Wang Lung. On the television set my teacher had rolled into the classroom that day, what I saw was apparently what white people thought Chinese people looked like: drab, with sharp cheekbones, slanted eyes narrowing to epicanthal folds, and vacant facial expressions that seemed to indicate a sort of feeblemindedness. It was humiliating. I could barely watch.

My eyes had been the brunt of jokes before. In middle school, I rode the school bus—or the "big yellow" as we called it—almost every day. Every morning the bus picked me up at the corner of Crumley and First Avenues, weaved its way through the streets of our suburb, and dropped me at General Wayne Middle School to streams of rambunctious kids funneling through the massive double doors to their lockers.

Sixth grade was rough. There was the science teacher, Mrs. Stevenson, who waited until the final parent-teacher conference at the end of the year to ask my mom if the reason I struggled in class was due to English being my second language. My mom was pissed. There was the bad judgment on my part to take rhythmics instead of weightlifting for PE—resulting in my having to dance in the gymnasium during Open House to Janet Jackson's "Black Cat," while twirling a ribboned wand in the air. There was the fact that I was first among my friends to get my period, and when we watched the filmstrip about our developing bodies and got to the part about menstruation, they all turned around in their desks to look at me, instantly informing everyone in the entire grade that I was ovulating.

And then there was the bus ride home. For some reason, a couple of older boys who weren't on my morning route were always on my afternoon bus, grabbing seats in the middle so they could taunt kids in front as well as behind them. I wasn't their only victim, but when I was their chosen target, I bore it all alone.

It's a chant that most Asian American kids have had to endure at one point or another: *Chinese, Japanese, dirty knees, look at these!* The two boys would turn around on the bus to face me, propped up on those dark green vinyl seat cushions that were always tearing, their white polyester guts pouring out. *Chinese*: they would pull the outer corners of their eyes up sharply, blurring their vision and laughing through their song. *Japanese*: they pulled their eyes sharply down. *Dirty knees*: a couple of quick pats on their legs. *Look at these*: they pinched their shirts at the nipples and pulled, mimicking a girl's breasts. And then they started with their spitballs, aiming the straws they had swiped from the school cafeteria right at my face. I would pull little, saliva-soaked balls of paper from my hair as my tormentors sat back down in their seats, not even pretending to suppress their laughter.

Blepharoplasty, also known as double eyelid surgery, is known to be the most requested cosmetic procedure in Asia, and the third most requested cosmetic procedure by Asian Americans.[1] The operation involves repositioning the patient's eyelid tissues and structures to create an eyelid crease. The transformation is from what they call a monolid to a double lid. Epicanthoplasty, which opens the inner corner of the eye by removing the epicanthal fold, is another common procedure among Asians. More than 90 percent of Asians—specifically East Asians and Southeast Asians—are estimated to be born with epicanthal folds, sections of skin at the eye's inner corner that extend vertically instead of toward the nose. Blepharoplasty and epicanthoplasty are often done in conjunction with one another to give a patient's eyes a "wider and brighter"[2] appearance. Because I was born with double eyelids and no epicanthal folds, I have often been told by other Asians just how lucky I am.

I support people pursuing elective surgery for whatever reason they choose. Our bodies are our bodies. I also believe that beauty standards and ideals are pervasive, limiting, and often dangerous. As someone born in Pennsylvania and taunted in my childhood for my slanted, almond-shaped eyes, I don't know what I'd elect to do had I been born with a monolid and epicanthal folds. I don't know if I would be unhappy with my reflection in the mirror, if I'd tug at my brows or pull up the inner corners of my eyes to see how an operation might help me achieve a wider and brighter appearance. What I do know is that I am not immune to the beauty standards defined by white femininity that have influenced generations past and present. I know that when Asians tell me how lucky I am to have the eyes I do, the compliment evokes in me some complex emotions. I also know that as much as some people may love my eyes, there are plenty of others who do not.

During the coronavirus pandemic, a new rash of anti-AAPI hate incidents rooted in centuries of anti-Asian racism once again swept across our nation and the world. As we sat isolated in our homes and neighborhoods, we began to hear the stories. A Thai grandfather viciously pushed onto the pavement as he went for his morning walk in San Francisco, resulting in fatal head injuries. A sixty-five-year-old Filipina woman punched and kicked outside a New York City apartment building while two doormen shut and locked the door instead of rushing to her aid. Four Korean women and two Chinese women brutally shot at massage parlors in the Atlanta area by a gunman who claimed he was trying to rid himself of his "sexual addiction." Between 2020 and the time of this writing, the national coalition Stop AAPI Hate has recorded more than 12,800 acts of hate against Asian Americans and Pacific Islanders in the United States. Countless other incidents remain unreported.

It's impossible to know just how many acts of hate have been endured by the AAPI community since COVID began, but in my family alone, we've experienced two. On June 14, 2020, my father was on his daily, early-morning walk through his beloved town of Sausalito, California. As he moved through the quiet streets lined with closed storefronts, signs hanging in their windows with messages like "Stay Safe" and "Sausalito Strong," a white woman strolled past him and said, "I hate Chinese people! Why do they come to this country?" As she continued to walk away, my dad was able to process what she had said and still in a state of shock, snapped a photo of her with his phone. He walked the rest of the way home, looking behind him every couple of minutes to make sure no one was following. When he safely reached his house, he told my mom what happened and then called me to do the same. With our encouragement, he filed a police report and recorded the incident on the Stop AAPI Hate website.

Then, on May 22, 2021, I was sitting alone outside an ice cream parlor in a town just south of my own when a man approached me spewing racial slurs. I could hear his rant from several yards away, and let's just say he was indiscriminate about whom he was targeting with his tirade. I kept my eyes locked on my phone, praying he would pass me by. But when he got to my table, he put his hands on the back of the empty chair opposite me. I could feel his hot breath on my face as he continued to yell. I quickly stood to seek safety inside the ice cream parlor. As I scurried to the door, an employee was already rushing out to my aid. He guided me through the entryway, quickly asked me if I was okay, and then placed his body between me and the aggressor. The employee asked the man to move along, said he would be calling the police, and then as the man fled, came inside to do just that. I did not choose to file a police report.

Amid all these hate incidents across the nation and in the life of my own family, I, like most Asian Americans, began to employ greater caution whenever I was out and about. I always felt safer when I was accompanied by my husband, who is white and over six feet tall. But whenever I found myself walking alone, I would do what I could to feel a little safer. I was always keenly aware of my surroundings. I moved to the other side of the street if I saw any man coming my way. If I didn't have that luxury, I would tighten my leg muscles, get my hands ready to brace a fall, clench my jaw, and tilt my head down to avoid eye contact. While my black hair is one indicator of my Asianness, it is my eyes that are the dead giveaway, especially when passing someone closely on a sidewalk. And so, I started to wear sunglasses whenever I had to walk alone, even on cloud-covered days. In that pandemic world, my double-lidded eyes that had been admired by many were now the thing I desperately kept hidden to preserve my life.

Once, in middle school, I invited a new friend over to our house. We lived in a modest split-level built in 1956 on a quarter acre, with a closed-in porch, shingled roof, and a brick chimney. Growing up in southeastern Pennsylvania, the Shaker-style aesthetic was prevalent, and my mother loved the practicality and simplicity of this traditional design. By the time I was hitting double digits, Mom had completely stripped from our home the heavy, autumnal hues of the 1970s and replaced them with a more delicate palette, clean and uncluttered. We had white walls, hardwood floors, and a sturdy dining room table situated in the center of a sunroom that was always bathed in light.

Mom was an exquisite painter, skilled in the style of *Trompe l'œil*, and her hand-painted furniture and framed art pieces could be found in every room of our house. I remember helping her stencil a twisted border of ivy onto the canvas doormats she sold at trade shows; my left hand struggled to hold down the stencil firmly enough so my shaky right hand wouldn't glob dark green paint outside the lines. Mom shrugged off my anxiety, saying, "It's fine. If you mess up, we'll just paint over it."

On summer days, we would slide open the window between the living room and the screened-in porch so the sound of whatever album my mom had put on the record player would pour out into the warm, sticky air where we sat sipping Country Time lemonade mixed from a powder. The Fifth Dimension, Bread, Carole King. My dad played his records too—Al Jarreau, James Taylor, Marvin Gaye—usually on Saturday mornings as he whipped up a batch of pancakes and cooked bacon in the microwave. He would line up the strips of bacon evenly on a plate atop a square of paper towel to absorb the grease, and then he served my brother and me two pieces each.

Weekend afternoons would find Dad working in the yard and Mom painting in her studio—an attic space my parents had renovated into a bright, airy room with skylights, a drafting table at its center with tubs of overflowing paintbrushes, tubes of acrylic paints, and canvases at every stage of completion were strewn everywhere. A wooden ramp that my mom had covered with vinyl sheeting in a white-tiled pattern led up to what was left of our attic space. I would use that vinyl-covered ramp as an indoor slide, making my mom's playground a magical playground of my own.

I was proud of our home—the perfect blend of traditional and contemporary American style. That day when I invited my new friend over to hang out after school, we got to my house and dropped our backpacks on the floor. When my friend looked up and took in her surroundings she said, wide-eyed, "Wow! This was not what I was expecting." I looked at her, confused. "It's just that I—," she stammered, "I expected to see, like, Chinese lanterns or dragons everywhere or something."

"Pfft," I vocalized this dismissive sound a little louder than I'd intended. "No, we don't have any of that," I said. "We're fully American."

Later, when I had told my mom what happened, she was defiant but proud. I remember feeling like we had shown that girl—Mom and I—and we would continue to show the next person, and every person after that, who we were and what we most certainly were not.

An immigrant to the United States from Singapore, my mom was only eight years old when she arrived in America. She went from being financially well-off in her country of birth where her family employed house staff and she and her three siblings all attended private school, to watching her parents work hard to thrive in New York City's Lower East Side. Her mother—my Po Po—was a renowned author who had published several books in China, as well as an accomplished musician and educator. Her father—my Gong Gong—was the new pastor at the Chinese Evangel Church on 29 East Broadway, right next door to the New York Public Library. His calling to shepherd that church was the reason they set sail for America. My mom and her three siblings had everything they needed, including two loving parents, but coming of age in the 1950s and '60s as Chinese immigrants couldn't have been easy. Her parents must have felt like they were caught up in a cultural whirlwind where they had to balance ethnic preservation and acculturation. My mom had to find her own way of *being* in a tumultuous time.

I remember only a handful of Chinese objects from my childhood home in Pennsylvania. In my parents' bedroom, Mom had some jewelry in her bureau, including a natural jade bangle. There were sets of *cloisonné* bowls in the kitchen cupboard and chopsticks in the utensil drawer. At Christmas, when we would haul out the decorations for the tree, I always found the collection of little Chinese lantern ornaments, each one adorned with a red silky tassel. I would play with them, dancing them upon my legs, their soft fringe undulating atop my knees. Somehow, the lanterns were always returned to their box on decorating day. We never put them up.

The house where I'm raising my own kids today would likely prompt the same surprised response in my middle school friend all those years ago. It is not conspicuously Chinese in its aesthetic. In fact, I've inherited quite a bit of my mom's design sensibility. My style might be described in today's interior design blogs as *minimalist bohemian* meets *modern farmhouse*. The walls are off-white, the floors are hardwood, and my product designer husband and I have invested in some signature pieces of furniture and artwork. But next to the dark walnut Eames Turned Stool is an antique Chinese pot that I carried home with me from a trip to visit our family village in Taishan in 1998. In my home office, Marvel Comics figurines stand in their action poses across from a set of hand-painted, ceramic Chinese dolls. Our kitchen cabinets contain plates from Anthropologie intermingled with Chinese enamel bowls, and our Crate & Barrel flatware shares space with a bundle of bamboo chopsticks passed down to me by my dad from the Chinese restaurant his family owned in Boston in the 1960s. If you open my closet, you will find Chinese-style jackets, dresses, and tops I've procured from Chinese shop owners and designers on Etsy. My bureau is burgeoning with earrings and bracelets featuring Chinese motifs, including a pair of gigantic dragon earrings that I bought to celebrate the Lunar New Year in 2024. If you follow the sound of the television to the family room downstairs, you might find us settling in for a family movie night where we now have the option of feasting our eyes on any number of films or shows made by and starring Asians.

One of the Christian Scripture texts that has entered mainstream public consciousness is the one where Jesus talks about the eye being the lamp of the body. It's found in the Gospel according to Matthew, who was known to be one of Jesus' twelve disciples. The passage goes like this: "The eye is the lamp of the body. So, if your eye is healthy, your whole body will be full of light, but if your eye is unhealthy, your whole body will be full of darkness. If, then, the light in you is darkness, how great is the darkness!" What Jesus seems to be saying is that if we keep our eyes open and attentive to our surroundings, we will be able to see the path before us. Our eye is like a lamp to a darkened path; it can show us the way. However, if our eyes are unhealthy or bad, they can lead us astray.

For our eyes to be the lamps through which light enters and emits from the body, one's head must be lifted. A flashlight pointed straight down onto the concrete never casts as large a glow as when it is tilted upward and forward. In this COVID-endemic world, I hold my head higher when I walk on the street. I am beginning to trust others enough to look them in the eye when we pass by each other. My body has released some of its trauma—something I've had to work on diligently through rest, recreation, therapy, and conversations with God and others. Unfortunately, what is true is that it will all come around again. It always does. There will be another virus. The United States will go to war with a country in Asia, and anyone in America who looks remotely Asian will suffer the consequences. A high-altitude, unidentified balloon will fly over the continent and people will start pointing fingers at the "Asian spies" who surely live in their neighborhoods, work in their offices, and go to school with their children.

I wonder what we as Asians will do then. Will we shift our gaze downward? Or lift our eyes like lanterns to face all that is before us?

NOTES

1. Nguyen, Marilyn Q., Patrick W. Hsu, and Tue A. Dinh. "Asian Blepharoplasty." Seminars in Plastic Surgery 23, no. 3 (2009): 185–197. https://doi.org/10.1055/s-0029-1224798.
2. Kenneth Kim, Dr., "Asian Eyelid Surgery in Los Angeles," Dream Medical Group, n.d., https://www.drkennethkim.com/procedure/eye/asian-eyelid-surgery/.

EARS

We all have those sounds that transport us somewhere. You hear it—a noise, a sonic pattern, a song—and for a moment you are somewhere else, a younger version of yourself reliving a moment permanently stamped by that auditory marker. A playlist of memories.

For me, the cascading coo of a mourning dove puts me in my childhood room in Pennsylvania, cuddled under my bedspread at dawn, right before my alarm clock sounds to warn me it's time to get up for school. I can see the weighted branches of the apple tree just starting to catch the morning light outside my window.

Phil Collins' 1990 hit "Do You Remember?" immediately takes me to the backseat of my parents' silver Nissan Stanza Wagon when I was a twelve-year-old crushing hard on the red-headed goalkeeper of my big brother's travel soccer team. The song pipes into the headphones from my bright yellow Sony Walkman, and my head leans against the window, taking in the passing landscape of farms and fields. I am forlorn and heartsick for a boy three years older than I am and way out of my league, but I allow myself to daydream as Phil croons that there was always something more important to say than "I love you."

And the soft ticktock of a clock—a sound that is less and less commonplace as the world goes digital—places me in the living room of our first single-family home. I am twenty-seven years old, and my newborn is fast asleep in her baby swing, tucked tightly into her swaddle. Her beloved binky has done its job and is now dangling from her parted, peaceful lips. I sit on our couch petting our dog, Ginger, and try not to make a single sound for fear of waking my daughter. I am exhausted but happy, and although the clock ticks, time seems to be standing still.

Some sounds take me to less desirable places. We all have those, too. The roar of a fast-approaching car with an unmuffled engine immediately hurls me into Lancaster, Pennsylvania, on a sunny day with my mom, dad, and brother on one of our regular visits to Amish Country to visit the wax museum and pick up a Shoofly pie from the Amish Farmers Market. As we walk along the sidewalk, a couple of young white men lean out the windows of their loud car and yell, "Dirty Chinks! Go back to where you came from!" I immediately fold myself into my dad's protective embrace; he tells my brother and me to ignore them while my lionhearted mom labors to resist her instinct to fight back.

Some sounds become native to our hearing, automatically rendering other sounds foreign. In my house growing up, we spoke only English. My parents could each speak some Chinese in the dialect their parents had spoken, but those were two different dialects so they couldn't use them to communicate with each other. Furthermore, they were raising two kids in southeastern Pennsylvania in the 1970s, '80s, and 90s, and so ensuring we were highly proficient in the English language, unadulterated by a second or third tongue, was a security blanket of sorts in which they generously sought to shroud us.

Sometimes we would go into Philadelphia's Chinatown as a family. When my mom got a hankering for "real" Chinese food or for groceries we couldn't find at Acme, we would drive into the city to walk around the brightly adorned and noisy streets, being sure to enter through the opulent China Gate at 10th and Arch. Chinatown was nothing like our neighborhood in the suburbs. The sidewalks and shops were congested and narrow. The people seemed impatient and pushy. Unlike the simplistic, Shaker-inspired aesthetic of our home, in Chinatown there was stuff *everywhere*. Bins overflowed with plastic trinkets. Crates were stuffed and stacked high with fruits and vegetables, many of which I didn't recognize. Window displays were covered top to bottom and left to right with merchandise and handwritten signs announcing the latest sale items. Behind fogged glass, roasted ducks hung in crowded bundles tied by their feet. Men sat atop boxes in alleyways behind restaurants, prepping food for the bustling kitchens inside, lit cigarettes dangling from the corners of their mouths. Elderly women wearing flimsy sandals shuffled up and down the street with so many bulging plastic bags hung over each wrist that I wondered how their arms didn't fall off their bodies.

The sounds of Chinatown were from another world entirely. Cantonese and Mandarin comingled as foreign chatter in my ears amid a cacophony of wind chimes and car horns. I remember walking past a storefront with my mother and being blasted by the careening melody of Chinese opera. The singer's voice was high-pitched and nasally, and I recall my mom and I laughing about how garish it sounded. Why the store owner felt the need to turn the volume up so obnoxiously high, I had no idea. I felt repelled by what I was hearing. But at least there were no white people around to whom I had to offer an embarrassed apology or explanation. In the midst of other Chinese people, however, I confess to feeling superior because my taste in music was "way better" than anything coming out of those Chinatown storefronts. Moments like these began to attune my young, impressionable ears to what was familiar versus foreign, acceptable versus rejectable, beautiful versus ugly.

I sat in class on the first day of high school, trying to prepare myself for what I knew was coming: a full day of enduring the uncomfortable experience of listening to each of my new teachers attempt to pronounce my name correctly.

"Marisa Navarro, Denise Nettle, Beth Newsome, Lauren . . . Nnnn . . . Nee . . . Nih . . . Nigh . . . Ning . . . Lauren Ning?"

"Here," I replied, slumping into my seat.

"Well, how do you pronounce it? Is it Ning?"

"It's (i)Ng. Like there's an 'i' in front of it." If I slid any further down, I'd be on the floor.

"Ahh, OK. What is that? Chinese?"

"Mhm." Please God, let this be over.

"All right then. Moving on. Ken Long, Billy O'Reilly, James Olson . . ."

The truth is, I gave my teachers an easy way out. All of us Ngs in America give everyone who tries to pronounce our surname the easy way out. My name is, in fact, correctly pronounced without a vowel sound. You just vocalize the consonants, producing the sound at the back of the throat rather than the front. But knowing how hard that is for most native English speakers in America, we just insert the "i" and call it a day.

Romanized versions of my Cantonese family name are Ang, Eng, Ing, and Ong. People with these surnames may share the same Chinese character as mine, but à la Vanna White, they have been handed a vowel (sometimes by immigration officers) to make their names more pronounceable for the American-born English-speaking tongue. The Mandarin version of Ng, again using the same Chinese character, is Wu. Let me tell you: *any* of these versions of my surname would have made things a lot easier growing up.

The sound of my teachers struggling to get my name right, and then ending on the pronunciation I'd provided with a reluctant tone as if they'd just been handed a third-place trophy, made me feel like my name was ugly. I remember reading books with characters who had romantic-sounding last names like Willoughby and Somerville. Their multiple syllables made them skip in your ear like a stone across a shimmering pond. In comparison, my name sounded like a rock that dropped into the water with one quick but heavy plunk. Much like the sound of that obnoxious Chinese opera singer, *Ng* was an auditory blight.

I remember walking with my dad one time and seeing a bunch of boxes on the sidewalk in front of a store, each marked "NG" in big black handwritten letters. "Look, Dad!" I said, excitedly, tugging on his hand, "Why is our name on all those boxes?" He looked down at the boxes, then at me, and said tenderly, "Store owners mark their unusable products as 'no good.' That's what that stands for, Princess. But don't worry; that's not our name."

But it was. It most certainly was.

By the time I was in my first semester at Oberlin College in the fall of 1996, intoxicating ideas and thrilling new ways of seeing the world were flitting into my psyche like the leaves that fell in droves from the trees in our main quad, Tappan Square. First, despite being in a small town in Ohio, there were more Asians at Oberlin than I had ever seen outside of Chinatown. My first roommate was a Korean girl from New Jersey, and there was even an Asia House dorm that I would visit for meals now and then at the invitation of friends who lived there. I signed up to be editorial staff for the Asian literary magazine, I enrolled in the introductory Mandarin language course, and after submitting a portfolio of my poetry to the creative writing program, I was accepted into my first writer's workshop.

My junior year I went to London for a semester with Oberlin's study abroad program. Our group was a combination of English and theater majors, accompanied by two professors. We studied social semantics, clutching John Berger's *Ways of Seeing* in our hands as we visited museums and historical sites, and we took in three theater performances a week at venues ranging from Shakespeare's Globe to pub theaters located at the farthest reaches of the Underground lines. Lots of things came together for me during that fall semester in London. I learned about imperialism, colonialism, white supremacy, and patriarchy, and the effects these systems of power have on marginalized communities. My brain was bursting at the seams with new knowledge and perplexing questions. It was a magical time, and I wished it would never end.

But someone was waiting for me at home. Daniel had been my boyfriend since our final year of high school. We met in art class—he did leatherwork while I painted large canvases with acrylics—and we ended up as senior prom dates. When I left for college, we worked hard to keep our long-distance relationship going strong while he remained in Pennsylvania. Mind you, this was in a time before cell phones. Email was just starting to take off. And so, we wrote each other long, handwritten letters and spent hours on the landline, racking up costly telephone bills. Our relationship had weathered distance and disagreements, but in London, I was faced with a challenge to our relationship that I hadn't anticipated: how could I be in a relationship with—let alone someday marry—a white man whose very existence embodied the oppressive systems I was learning to reject and dismantle?

One chilly night in October, I sat on the stairs inside the Gower Street flat I shared with five other students. The coiled telephone cord stretched tautly from the wall of our galley kitchen to the receiver I held tightly against my ear. Daniel was on the other end of the line, in his Philadelphia apartment, 3,500 miles away and five hours behind. "We can't be together," I said quietly. "It won't work."

"But it can," he replied desperately. "I'll do whatever it takes."

I pushed back. Hard. I went on a tirade about the Madame Butterfly Effect, Miss Saigon, and the exotification and objectification of Asian women in the white male imagination. Daniel listened. I denounced Orientalism and the centuries of looting and plundering that resulted in the objects I'd seen on display at the British Museum earlier that day—art and artifacts that belonged back in the countries they were stolen from. He listened. I told him he had no idea the magnitude of his white privilege and that he needs to read Peggy McIntosh's essay "Unpacking the Invisible Knapsack" if he was even going to begin to understand. He said he would absolutely read it. I warned him that if we ever had kids, they would be half Chinese and he would understand race and ethnicity in a way he never had, and he would need to be ready. Like, really freaking ready. Daniel listened to it all.

The next day, he booked his flight to London for my fall break. It would be the first time we'd seen each other in months and his first-ever trip over the Atlantic Ocean. When he arrived at my flat, he unfolded his xeroxed copy of Peggy McIntosh's article and showed me his notes, scribbled all over the text and crammed into the margins. My life experiences traveling abroad were irrevocably changing me, and in that moment, it was clear they were changing him too. Less than three years later, we were married.

Originally, I planned to take Daniel's surname as my own and either make Ng an additional middle name or retire it altogether. I began using the name Kushner when introducing myself and changed my Comcast email address accordingly. But when the time came to make the change official after our wedding, something didn't feel right. I realized I had spent my childhood and adolescence wishing my name away, shrinking down into my seat whenever someone butchered its pronunciation, imagining what romance might come my way if only it contained a couple more syllables or a breathy vowel, and unable to shake the belief that it really was "No Good." But, after years of advanced studies, exploring the world, and working diligently to unpack the invisible knapsack of internalized racism I had been carrying for so many years, I could no longer imagine parting ways with my name. Ng was the only one of my three names with Chinese origin, and now that I had the chance, I didn't want to let it go. When I thought about who I was, I didn't feel like a *Lauren Lisa Kushner*; I felt like a *Lauren Lisa* Ng.

I asked Daniel if he was OK with me not taking his name, and he didn't skip a beat in expressing his support. In that moment I remembered a campaign poster I had made my junior year in high school when I ran for class president and won. It read, "NG. Two letters. No vowels. Deal with it." Back then, I had the confidence to tell others to accept my name just as it is. Years later, I finally had the confidence to embrace it for myself.

There's this thing my parents used to do for me (and my brother) when I was a kid. One of them would read me a bedtime story, tuck me in, and then tell me to lie on my side with my head directly under the light of the bedside lamp. They would lay a tissue on my shoulder and, using a thin metal rod with a tiny spoon-like scoop at the end, they'd clean each of my ears, carefully removing the sticky wax and depositing the detritus onto the tissue. This was one of my absolute favorite things in the entire world. I would beg my parents to clean my ears with this Chinese ear cleaner almost every night, and one of them would say, "Honey, I just cleaned your ears a few days ago. They're not dirty yet!"

"It's okay," I would plead, with a sweet look on my face. "Even if nothing comes out, you can just scratch inside my ears! Please? It feels so good!"

Sometimes they relented, and I would lie there in my cozy bed, eyes closed, while my mom or dad carefully ran the scoop around the curves of my ear, stopping to scratch continuously in a certain spot if I cooed, "Ooh, ooh, that spot right there. . . ." I would be half asleep when they'd say, "Turn over," and I'd flip to the opposite side to give them access to my other ear. By the time they finished that one, I would be just awake enough to feel them kiss my cheek and hear them click off the lamp as they whispered goodnight.

I've introduced all three of my children to the Chinese ear cleaner. They're like me when I was young; each one begs for this ritual more often than is needed, and each one nearly falls asleep as I gently trace the tiny canyons of their ears with the metal scoop. My husband has never let me use it on him, despite being married to me for almost twenty-five years. I suppose it looks a little intimidating, considering most of us American-born kids were told by our doctors not to put even a cotton swab in our ears for fear of losing our hearing. I've asked Daniel many times to reconsider, as the pleasure of cleaning a loved one's ears is almost as euphoric for me as being the one whose ears are getting cleaned. It is an act of utmost intimacy, of trust, and of love.

Once, I posted a photo of my ear cleaner on Facebook and captioned it: *IYKYK*. A bunch of my Asian friends immediately chimed in with their comments. *Best feeling ever! Ours is made of bamboo. Ah, the memories of sitting still under the lamp!* Several of my non-Asian friends were curious about what it was, throwing out guesses and asking for answers. *Please reveal its purpose! I'm dying to know!* A few friends who are married to Asian partners said they knew what it was but were still too skittish to try it for themselves.

I never once thought of our family's ear cleaner as a foreign object that had no business going near the ear, much less inside the ear canal. It was introduced to me as a child as an instrument of pure delight used in an act of unfettered love. I realize now that, while I am still in the act of *becoming* Chinese—of reclaiming and celebrating my ethnicity, Asian culture, and heritage—my memories are riddled with reconciled moments of being both fully Chinese and fully American.

These moments are woven together, seamless. They don't run parallel in my mind but occupy the same course. Dad cradling me in his arms in front of my drawn window, the moon shining as he sings to me, *Twinkle twinkle, little star, how I wonder what you are.* Falling blissfully asleep while Mom gently cleans my ears, taking her time even when the cleaning part is long completed. Snuggling under my covers, clutching my favorite stuffed animals, my belly full of a hearty dinner of Hamburger Helper as Mom clicks off my bedroom light. Dad whispering, *Goodnight, Princess. Sweet dreams.*

These are the sounds of a world I know. Familiar, native, congruent. My Chinese and American identities interwoven in my ears. A harmonious blend that only sounded out of tune when listening to the voices that called me a stranger and an alien. A hard-fought peace as I've learned there is nothing foreign that someone else hasn't put there.

NOSE

My dad traveled a lot for work while I was growing up. As executive staff for the American Baptist Churches USA—the Christian denomination through which both he and I are ordained ministers—his job took him all over the country, and sometimes abroad, for conferences and church-related events. Dad boarded a plane at least once a month. There was even an annual board meeting he had to attend every June that always started the Monday after Father's Day. This meant he would fly out on Saturday so he could arrive at his destination with enough time to prepare for the meeting. Every year my mom would get cards for my brother and me to sign and decorate, and we placed them in Dad's suitcase for him to open alone in his hotel room.

I missed my dad terribly when he traveled. He was always a ready playmate when I was a child, and he filled our home with a steady ease that made me feel safe and comforted. He also reveled in spoiling me, his younger child and only daughter. When he was home, I could easily get him to take me for ice cream or donuts since his love for sweets surpassed my own. When he returned from a business trip, he would call my brother and me down to the living room to give us our souvenirs: a stuffed bear from California, a toy racecar from Indianapolis, a chunk of fool's gold from Colorado, a scorpion lollipop from Arizona, a sand- and glitter-filled keychain from Florida. I would sit on Dad's lap to open my gift as he told the story of exactly where he found the treasure and why he picked it out just for me. I know the promise of these gifts made his traveling easier for each of us.

My ritual the night before each of his trips was to sit on his bed while he packed his suitcase. Freshly bathed, my hair still damp, I would curl up in his bedspread as he folded dress shirts and slacks, rolled up his neckties, and selected a handkerchief for each day. At first, I would be happy, grilling him about the details. *Where are you going this time? Watcha gonna do there? When are you coming back?* But as he neared the end of his task, just as he closed the top of his suitcase to zipper it shut, I would start to cry.

One night, as my tears devolved into desperate pleading for him not to leave, my dad reached for one of his favorite handkerchiefs and handed it to me. I held the midnight blue square of soft cotton in my hands, running my finger along its thin-lined brown border.

"I want you to keep this," he said. "Then whenever you miss me, you can hug it because it smells like me."

I brought the handkerchief to my nose and inhaled; it did smell like my father: the scent of a cleanly shaven face, of comfortable clothes that have just transitioned from crisp to well-worn, of spiced cologne that evoked his intellect and humility, with notes of Motown and folk. I named it *Hanky*, and from that moment on, I slept with it against my face every night, even when Dad was home.

A couple of years later, Hanky had become so threadbare that Dad had to give me a second handkerchief. This one was light blue, and while I loved it, I couldn't bring myself to say goodbye to the original. On the night before his next trip, Dad said, "Watch this!" He spread the new hanky flat on my bed as he was saying goodnight to me. He rolled up what was left of the tattered Hanky and placed it on top, then began to roll both squares of fabric—the old inside the new—like an egg roll. He tucked in the final corner and placed it, snug and compact, onto my pillow. I breathed in the scent of my dad once again and drifted off to sleep.

At some indeterminable point, a scent—like a sound—goes from being foreign to familiar. At yet another point, the familiar becomes so engraved into olfactory memory that you become capable of time travel. When my husband and I started dating our senior year of high school, his scent was intoxicating to me. When he picked me up in his 1986 maroon Toyota Celica hatchback, we would drive to one of our favorite parks where we lowered his backseat and crawled into the now spacious trunk, the hatch wide open so we could stargaze. Wrapped in blankets, we kissed for hours, and eventually I would fall asleep nuzzled into the slope of his neck, breathing him in deeply.

Daniel's scent—slightly musky but bright, like the moment you unzip your tent on a quiet, dewy morning and step out into the awakening forest—hasn't changed in the thirty years I've known him. Now that he is in his late 40s, one of his more recent fashion picks has been the shacket: a half-shirt, half-jacket outerwear item that can go from bumming around indoors on a lazy Saturday to traipsing around town to run some errands. He has four different shackets, but there's one I am particularly prone to stealing. It is lined with a soft fleece, and it's the one that smells like him the most. I'll grab it from his closet from time to time and wrap myself in the scent of this man who has been by my side since we were kids. I begin my time travel and find myself back in his Celica, our legs entwined, staring up at the night sky. I travel to the moment he got down on one knee and asked me to marry him. I travel to that day in the hospital when he rocked me back and forth in his arms, laboring with me as we awaited the birth of our first child. I travel to just days ago, when while brushing my teeth in the early morning, he came up behind me, wrapped his arms around my waist, and kissed me on the slope of my neck. Daniel's aroma is still intoxicating, but in a different way than when I was seventeen. Back then, his scent was foreign but invigorating. Now it's familiar and comforting like the circadian sun, warming all my adult memories.

There are other scents that transport me through time. Every now and then I detect something on a breeze—it's usually in cool weather, always outside, and in a semi-populated area. It's the smell of my Ngin Ngin's kitchen, but it doesn't smell like any specific food. It's just the smell of her kitchen late at night, when the cooking was over, the dishes were washed, and the plastic tablecloth was wiped down with a sponge and some soapy water. The scent departs as quickly as it arrives, but for that moment, I am right there, sitting at her kitchen table as the lights throughout the house turn off, one by one.

When I recall my childhood, other prominent scents come to mind: cooked apples drenched in cinnamon and sugar as my mom, wearing her holiday apron, stirred them in the steaming pot; *lap cheong* (Chinese pork and chicken sausage) sizzling and plump on the pan, waiting to be mixed into my dad's signature fried rice; freshly cut grass suspended in air so humid you could hold its weight; wet macadam after a summer storm, acrid like burning rubber; an herby and aromatic pot roast cooking for hours in the oven on a wintry day; Mom's acrylic and oil paints, freshly stretched canvas, and turpentine filling her artist's studio with sharp fumes; Italian hoagies smothered in oil, vinegar, oregano, and sweet yellow peppers that our church's youth group assembled and delivered to homes as a fundraiser every Super Bowl Sunday; fresh cassette tape ribbon and the plastic wrapping on new CDs, metallic and resinous as I excitedly anticipated the latest addition to my music library; stale sticks of sugary but otherwise flavorless pink gum inside baseball card packs that left white powder everywhere; the artificially sweet smell of berries on my Strawberry Shortcake dolls and My Little Ponies; my brother's sweaty shin guards; my mom's Oil of Olay, and my dad's freshly laundered handkerchiefs.

While my family regularly ate Chinese food, I didn't necessarily think of it as such. My parents would pepper Chinese dishes into our repertoire without any fanfare, so in my mind, *lap cheung* fried rice was no different than spaghetti and meatballs. It was just another dish. I remember eating out as a family at a new Chinese restaurant that had just opened in our neighborhood. As I looked through the menu, my eye caught on something astonishing. I turned to my mom and exclaimed, "Look, Mom! They make your beef and broccoli here!"

While we always had leftover Chinese food in the refrigerator, the school lunches my dad packed for me never included any. Instead, he made me a bologna sandwich on white bread, with a thin layer of mayonnaise spread all the way to the edges just as I liked it. Sometimes, if he had the energy and time, he would make my favorite egg salad with little flecks of paprika. Those were always good days at school, when I looked forward to eating that egg salad sandwich all morning during class. At lunchtime, I would untuck my sandwich from the folded plastic bag—we were too cheap to purchase actual ziplock bags, so we bought the ones that had a fold-over top—and devoured it along with the potato chips and green grapes my dad had packed. I washed it all down with chocolate milk purchased from the cafeteria line. My parents never asked me if I wanted to bring Chinese food to school. If they had, I probably would have said no. At that age—and at that time—I wasn't interested in doing anything that made me stand apart from my peers, none of whom were Chinese.

One Christmas break when my brother was in middle school and I was still in elementary school, our family packed up the car to visit my Ngin Ngin in Boston. My parents did all the work loading our luggage and gifts for my grandmother, aunt, and cousins who all lived together in the same house.

Greg and I only had to worry about ourselves: packing a book to read, our favorite stuffed animals, and our Walkmans, cassette tapes, and headphones for the long, six-hour drive up I-95. A couple of hours into our road trip, Greg and I alerted our parents that we were hungry for dinner. We were excited, whispering across the backseat armrest about all the delicious restaurants where we might stop. This was the interstate after all, where fast-food options abounded. Would it be McDonalds? Arby's? Roy Rogers? Wendy's? We could sure go for a chocolate Frosty and French fries. We waited with anticipation for Dad to pull into the next rest stop, knowing better than to make our preferences known. But still, we could taste the glorious grease and imagine what toys we might find inside our kids' meals.

Finally, Dad took an offramp that led to a rest area, and there it was: the big, red bubble letters sandwiched neatly between two golden buns. We were having Burger King for dinner! We were clambering out of our seatbelts when my dad pulled into the neon-lit parking lot and turned off the ignition. As we went to open our doors, Dad turned to us in the backseat.

"Kids, we're just using the bathrooms. We're not eating here."

"WHAT?!" Greg and I practically shouted in unison, but then quickly held our tongues.

Dad looked at us sternly, and then, his face softening, he smiled.

"I made fried rice! Just go use the bathroom, and then we'll come back to the car and eat."

My brother and I must have been a sorrowful sight. Our shoulders slumped, we followed my parents into the Burger King, walked straight to the bathroom, and then back out of the restaurant. Greg and I tortured ourselves, looking up at the bright menu above the counter, then down to the families waiting in line, with kids excitedly awaiting their burgers, chicken tenders, fries, and kids' meal prizes. Back at the car, my dad retrieved from the trunk his homemade fried rice, perfectly portioned into four plastic containers. As we sat inside the car and peeled open the lids, the familiar aroma of *lap cheung*, fluffy egg, green peas, sautéed onion, and tender white rice plumed. It was blistering cold outside, so the windows of our car quickly fogged from our steaming dinners. I just knew the smell of the fried rice was emanating forcefully from our car, despite the doors being closed, so I was grateful for the privacy of our fogged-up windows as white families got in and out of their cars nearby, unable to place where the strange scent was coming from. I sank deep down into my seat, worrying about what they'd think if they saw a Chinese family shoveling rice into their mouths in a Burger King parking lot.

Unlike me with my suburban Pennsylvanian upbringing in the 1980s and early '90s, my three children have been raised in the San Francisco Bay Area in the 2010s and 2020s. Sushi, bibimbap, poke bowls, and boba tea are choices as prevalent among kids and teenagers as are burgers, fries, and milkshakes. When I packed homemade vegetable sushi rolls in my son's school lunch, his friends wouldn't hold their noses; they ambushed him and begged him to share. When my daughter was in elementary school, I volunteered to bring in Chinese treats to celebrate the Lunar New Year. Handing out squares of my homemade *nian gao*, I watched some children pop it right into their mouths, delighting in the chewy, sticky-sweet consistency. Others sniffed it, nibbled a bit off the edge, and then politely placed it back on their paper plate saying, "No, thank you." I couldn't help contrasting this with what I experienced when I was growing up, when anything "ethnic" smelled foreign and out of place. What a difference thirty years and 3,000 miles can make.

In 2019, Daniel and I took the kids to London for a post-Christmas vacation. We loaded up the car and drove to the San Francisco airport. Hours later, we boarded our plane, heading for London's Heathrow. These were the years when

I had to have several tricks up my sleeve to keep the kids occupied on long travel days. I packed each of them surprises in their carry-on backpacks: coloring books, glow sticks, travel board games, a new doll, and some treats they didn't usually get at home. We were an hour or so into our flight when the beverage and snack cart rolled by, and my middle daughter asked if we could buy something.

"No need," I said, as I reached down for the bag I had tucked under the seat in front of me. I pulled out a large plastic bag, revealing a plastic container of my dad's fried rice. He had come to our house the night before and offered to cook dinner for us as we were busy packing our bags for the trip. Earlier that morning, as I went through the refrigerator, throwing out items that wouldn't last the two weeks of our absence, I found the leftover fried rice and thought about how delicious it would taste when we were on the plane, hungry for a hearty, hot meal.

Now, as my kids saw me portioning out the fried rice into the paper bowls I had packed, they squealed with delight. "No wayyyy," said my eldest as her eyes widened with excitement. The mouthwatering aroma filled our row and began to permeate the entire plane. I passed each bowl with a plastic spoon to my husband, who placed them into our children's eager hands. A couple of people peered over their seats into our row. They may have been annoyed by the foreign smell. They may have been jealous of a familiar favorite. Either way, it didn't matter to me. I scooped up a heaping spoonful of the steaming rice and dug in.

MOUTH

The first funeral I attended was for my Gong Gong, when I was five years old. My memories of my mom's father are an indiscernible blend of actual and projected impressions from seeing photos of us together in the years since his death: Gong Gong bouncing me on his knee. Gong Gong carrying me in his arms and planting a kiss on my right cheek. Gong Gong taking me from room to room in the New York City apartment he shared with my Po Po and posing me like a doll in each one. In my favorite photograph from this series, I stand atop my grandparents' bed with a blank but trusting stare, my tiny pigtails and rippling thigh rolls on display. I alone was the subject of these photos; my grandfather was the one behind the camera, unseen but viscerally present in the way he framed each shot, with me—his newest pride and joy—posed at the center. My mom says that, at his funeral, we went up as a family of four to view him in his open casket. As she tells it, I tugged on her hand and said, "Mommy, the smiley part of Gong Gong has gone away."

Chinese tend to approach the reality of death with a candor and directness that can be jarring to some. Our elders speak freely about the inconvenient, uncomfortable realities of aging. Grandparents will often share the discomfiting details of their recent hernia surgery as readily as they will release a hearty belch or noxious fart while still seated at the dinner table. They will not even acknowledge these emissions, even as their grandchildren exchange awkward glances and giggles. I recently took my ninety-two-year-old godfather out to lunch for his birthday, and over a plate of *japchae*, he ran down the list of all his friends who had died since our last visit together. His words carried a tone of sober pragmatism, but I still noticed a shimmer at the corners of his eyes. Also comfortable with the realities of their mortality, my own parents have already taken me and my brother, our spouses, and all six of their grandchildren to see their future burial sites. On that windy day when we visited the cemetery, I peered down into the fog-dripped valley from the rocky California hillside, listening while my mom and dad acted as docents, proudly showing us where their cremated remains are destined to become one with the earth.

I've been to quite a few Chinese funerals. At many of them, mourners are handed a small white envelope as they depart from the service. Inside is a piece of candy and a shiny coin, symbolic gifts for loved ones as they go forward from their time of communal grieving. I remember opening these envelopes as a child and often being delighted to find my favorite golden-wrapped butterscotch inside. My mom would gently touch my shoulder and nod her head, instructing me to unwrap and eat the candy on the spot. I'd watch as others—young and old—would place a candy into their mouths, nodding respectfully to the family of the deceased as they exited the building. This Buddhist ritual, adopted by many Chinese regardless of their religious beliefs, introduces some sweetness to balance out the bitterness of death.

My family has long been known to have an unparalleled penchant for sweets. When I was growing up, my parents put dessert on the table after both lunch and dinner, every single day. Our freezer was always stocked with popsicles and gallon tubs of Turkey Hill ice cream. We had an Entenmann's Bakery outlet store close to our house, so there was always a discounted, iced fudge cake on the kitchen counter, as well as a variety box of their donuts: chocolate frosted, glazed, and crumb topped. Our pantry was continuously stuffed with cookies and candy—a practical benefit of Mom being our church's youth group leader, which I thoroughly enjoyed. Even if we had no other indulgences in the house, my dad would cut some fresh fruit and put it on the table after the meal. "Gotta have something sweet," he would say.

I didn't realize my family was distinctive in our daily need for sweets until I was in college. I was eating out with some friends, and when I was the only one to ask to see a dessert menu, I mentioned that I was used to having something sweet after every lunch and dinner. They looked at me, astonished. Not only did their families only eat dessert on special occasions, but that was the norm, and my family was most definitely the exception. I was stunned. I went on a fact-checking mission and asked my best friends from high school. "Yup," they replied, "it's just the Ng family that eats dessert twice a day. That's part of why we always loved coming to your house!" To this day, desserts remain part of my everyday life. I inherited my dad's sweet tooth and my mom's language of showing love through the gift of homemade pastry. Even if it's just some fresh fruit or a small square of dark chocolate, I always finish off my meal with something sweet.

More than twenty years ago, I went vegan and eliminated all animal products from my diet. It was hard at first to find plant-based desserts to satisfy my twice-daily hankering, but I quickly learned to recreate some of my favorite treats from childhood—my life story told through sweets. I whipped up vegan chocolate cakes, fruit pies, and my own take on popular candy bars. I would pick up my kids from school carrying a basket of vegan Rice Krispies treats, fudgy brownies, or lemon squares for them to share with their friends. My mom was the one, however, who veganized all my favorite Chinese desserts so I could enjoy them once again.

Like lots of Chinese kids, *don tot* (sweet egg custard) was my go-to treat as a child. Whenever our family took a trip into Philadelphia's Chinatown, my brother and I would always enjoy them warm, right out of the bakery oven. As soon as my dad placed the radiating metal tin in my hands, my mouth would start to water. We visited my Ngin Ngin (my dad's mother) in Boston every year after Christmas, and she would always have a pink Chinese bakery box filled with *don tot*, waiting for our arrival. I would sit in her kitchen in my pajamas, stretching my legs out after a six-hour drive, and the flaky crust of the *don tot* combined with the silky, sweet custard was as comforting as being tucked into a warm bed. Over the last few years, my mom has perfected the vegan *don tot*. It tastes like my childhood but incorporates new ingredients to comply with my adult convictions. I joke with her that she and I should open a vegan Chinese bakery with the *don tot* as our signature item. She always replies, "Nah, too much work. I just want to make them for you."

I ask my mom to share her recipes for the revised vegan versions of my favorite desserts. She gladly sends them, but I have yet to recreate any. It could just be laziness on my part, but I suspect it has something more to do with the way the gift of her desserts makes them taste in my mouth. Like new history being passed down from one generation to the next. Like a sweet story spoken just for me.

I remember one night when I was in high school, my parents and I sat around the dinner table for a late meal. My brother was off at college, and I had returned home after a tiring field hockey practice. As my dad and I cleared the dishes and brought them to the sink, my mom brought out a Pepperidge Farm devil's food cake—a decadent, three-layer chocolate cake that she had pulled from the freezer an hour prior so it would be thawed and ready to eat after dinner. My eyes widened with excitement. We had been enjoying our dessert for about three minutes when Dad looked at the empty cake box sitting on the table and asked, "Why do they have to call it devil's food cake?"

"Because it's the opposite of angel food cake," Mom replied.

"But why does it have to be seen as evil just because chocolate is dark?"

Mom rolled her eyes.

"I'm tired of dark things being labeled as evil and light things being labeled as good. It's racist," said my dad.

"Stop it," replied my mom. "It's just what they call it. It's just cake."

"But the archetype of color is a thing," Dad persisted. "And this messaging is racist."

For the first time ever, I watched my dad push his dessert away from him, refusing to finish his slice of cake. My mom rolled her eyes again, but I could tell she was intrigued by the conversation. After all, the two of them had met in college when they got into a fight about racialized identity. Soon after, they started meeting up to coauthor the constitution for a new Asian Dragon Society club at their school.

The devil's food cake conversation was a pivotal moment for me. By debating over our dessert, my parents taught me that critical discourse could—in fact, should—be part of a family's daily life together. I was being taught to analyze the world around me for a widened perspective and for the benefit of others. I was being taught that resistance can take on many forms, including pushing away a piece of chocolate cake, and that sometimes sweetness and bitterness can commingle in the same mouthful.

When they set sail from Singapore to immigrate to the United States in August 1958, my mom's family voyaged for more than a month, traveling to Hong Kong, then to the Philippines, and then to Japan before finally boarding their American ship in Yokohama. The U.S.S. President Wilson carried my mom, her three younger siblings, and her parents first to Honolulu, and then to San Francisco where, in the brisk September air, she and her brother rushed to the ship's deck as the looming, rust-red Golden Gate Bridge passed above them. From far away, my mom had feared the bridge would graze the top of her head, but now, as she looked up beneath it in eight-year-old awe, the iconic steel and concrete structure heralded her arrival from a bewildering height, as if trumpeting a promise of momentous things to come.

I was twenty years old and in college when my mom finally told me that story. We were standing at a rocky viewpoint overlooking the Golden Gate and its glistening bay. She and my dad had recently moved back to California after two decades living on the east coast. I had said goodbye to my childhood home in Malvern, Pennsylvania, and started flying out to the Bay Area for my college breaks instead. That day, Mom had taken me to lunch and then drove us up to the Marin Headlands to see the bridge from its most breathtaking vantage point accessible by foot. From this national recreation area, you can see the full expanse of the Golden Gate from its northern point in Sausalito to its southern point in San Francisco.

After hearing my mom share what it had been like to watch as the bridge got closer and closer, fearing she would have to duck down to avoid being struck by its mass, I went back to school reflecting on why it had taken so many years for her to tell me that story. For my very next creative writing assignment at Oberlin College, I wrote a poem about her experience, and I titled it "The End of Nothing." In it, I muse:

> Now, an image, a single
> word of history, wrapping
> a piece of the earth.
>
> The earth is naked.
> We lose a word per second.
> We'll spend forever recovering them
> for they have no beginning.

I wondered about other stories my mother had not yet told me. Was it because she wasn't ready? Was it because I hadn't asked? I thought about the words I might yet be able to shake free from my mother. I thought about the words my daughter might one day have to shake free from me.

I suppose we all take part in the revising of history, whether we mean to or not. There are things we omit, sometimes by choice or sometimes because we simply forget. There are things we modify, often out of compassion or shame. There are things we introduce, perhaps out of sadness, or for added humor, or to instill hope.

At a recent family reunion, I asked my brother if he remembered the time we got so mad at each other that he threw a badminton racquet at my face. He swore zero recollection of the incident. Did it happen or didn't it? Did it happen differently than I remember, and that's why his memory isn't being triggered? One memory we do share, up to a point, is of the day he chased down a guy who was bullying me during my freshman year in high school. Greg—a high school senior at the time—got one of his buddies to join him in his car after school while I sat in the backseat. We tailed the guy's school bus, my brother and his friend staring him down menacingly with every stop as the bully looked out at them from the back door of the bus, clearly intimidated. When the guy finally had no choice but to get off the bus, he fled, sprinting across a field. Greg said, "Lau, wait here," and he and his friend took off in hot pursuit. This is the point at which our memories diverge. Greg remembers chasing down the kid and giving him a stern talking-to; I remember seeing my hero grab a villain by the collar, lifting the guy inches off the ground before placing him back down on his feet so he could scurry off, never to bother me again.

History is revised and distilled by each of us, with each passing moment. The sharp details of our present experience start to round around the edges with time, like rocks smoothed by lapping waves. Eventually, highly nuanced and complex events can fit onto a few pages in a diary, and then, into a rudimentary anecdote via text message. There's an anthropological reason for this: Our brains need to continuously free up space. But I think we also do it to maintain a sense of agency amid the vast storehouses of our memory. We keep what we want to keep; we shelve what we don't want to deal with now but may want to access later; we jettison what we refuse to pass on to our children.

As I write this memoir, our American culture is enamored with the idea of full disclosure. Every day there is a fresh news article or Netflix docuseries featuring a tell-all or exposé that promises to serve up intel you've not heard before. We are told that to be our authentic selves, we need to be uncensored, and that to be in authentic community, nothing should be held back. Traditional Chinese culture stands in contrast, with value being placed on discretion. Chinese values teach us to say less to protect family and preserve honor. As a second-generation Chinese American, I find myself somewhere in the middle. I believe honesty and integrity are important, but I think each can be upheld in silence, just as much as through sound. I think that when my mom waits twenty years to tell me something, it's because that is the precise moment in which it was always meant to be shared. I think that when two people remember things differently, it's because two different lives were being lived. I think that when we spice up our memories with new details, dilute them to smooth out the sharpness of their bite, or sweeten them like a butterscotch candy to a bitter palate, it's okay, because memory—like a taste upon the tongue—is powerful for how it impacts us in the present moment.

Recently, one of my children was going through a life-threatening crisis. The morning after the situation had reached its peak, I awoke after three hours of fitful sleep, in tears. I texted my mom: *Can you come over today?* She quickly replied. *Yes. I'll be over in an hour.* I was sitting at my dining room table, my head in my hands, when I heard her come through the front door. She greeted our dog with gentle words. I heard her take off her shoes. She walked down the steps to where I was, rested her arms on my shoulders, and placed a tray of her homemade *don tots* on the table. I wept as she stood behind me and then laid her head against mine, sweetness atop bitterness, sweetness atop bitterness.

BELLY

My first formal encounter with Traditional Chinese Medicine (TCM) was on a family trip to China in 1998. Our two-week itinerary included a visit to a hospital where TCM practitioners led us in a demonstration on ways we could rectify the imbalance in our *qi*—the vital life force that keeps all the dimensions of our being in balance. Holding hands in a large circle around the room, we experienced *qi gong*, murmuring our amazement as a steady electrical current pulsed through each of us. My parents bought my brother an herbal acne treatment that promised to clear up his skin in a matter of days (which it did!). My aunt and cousins stocked up on other natural remedies for a variety of ailments. Everything was about restoring balance between the *yin* and *yang*: opposite yet complementary forces that lead to good health when our bodies hold them in equal proportion. *Yin* is the feminine force, the dark side of the well-known symbol, and is associated with coolness and cold. *Yang* is its masculine counterpart, the light side of the circle, and is associated with warmth and heat. The TCM practitioners advised us about the things we should do, contemplate, and consume when we need more *yin* to balance our *yang*, or vice versa.

I learned something about this balance from my grandmother. She spoke only in Cantonese, but I always understood her intent when she pushed a certain food toward me and urgently motioned her fingers to her mouth: *eat, eat*. My

Ngin Ngin could tell if I was running hot or cold, and she would try to make it right by feeding me foods rich in the opposite energy. I especially recall pungent broths in earthy, unappetizing shades, swimming with indiscernible bits that I knew were somehow good for me. Sometimes these broths were hot; other times they were cold. I would take tiny sips, wanting to be obedient, and then smile to say I was starting to feel better.

My mom also tried to help me achieve balance, but with foods I recognized. When my belly hurt, she sat me on the couch downstairs in front of the TV and brought an endless supply of ice-cold ginger ale. If I was lucky, she served it to me with a bendy straw. When I was stuffy and sneezing, she made me a bowl of Lipton's chicken noodle soup from a packet—the one with the noodles that weren't short but weren't quite long either, as if they were factory leftovers from a more premium product. I would slip in and out of sleep on that family room couch, morning cartoons fading to afternoon soap operas, then to after-school specials, as my *qi* slowly came back into balance.

It is a well-known fact that Chinese parents like to feed their children. For some, this is based on the belief that a child with a full belly is a child experiencing prosperity and good fortune. In many cases, food is a way of showing love in a culture that doesn't often do so with words or physical affection. Regardless of the reason, Chinese families tend to go overboard when it comes to food, which is interesting considering Chinese approach many things in life with a great deal of austerity and restraint.

For example, my parents taught me to always prepare double the amount of food I might need. This took a while for my husband to get used to. I'll cook five cups of rice when only our son is eating dinner with us that night, fully recognizing there will be a lot left over. The visual of a rice cooker brimming with a steaming bed of fragrant, fluffy white grain in the pot makes me feel happy—blissful even—and confirms I am doing my job as a mother to provide. It would be unacceptable to ration our portions or worry about having enough for everyone to have second helpings. In a world where so much is lacking, I want my family's plates to be heaping with food, and I want leftovers in the fridge for their lunches the next morning.

My practice of preparing double is especially critical if hosting guests for a meal. Recently, when we were expecting a couple for dinner, I set a pot of water to boil for pasta. I asked Daniel how much penne I should prepare, and the sweet man did the math to answer me, fully knowing I wouldn't listen. "Well, the box says it serves eight," he said. "And there are only four of us eating, so. . . ."

"Hand me that second box," I nodded. Daniel did so without contest. I poured a box and a half of penne into the boiling water.

This compulsion is not just about making sure there is enough for everyone to eat; it's also about a spirit of generosity. When my guests see overflowing dishes on the dining table and watch as I return to the kitchen again and again to refill them from what seems to be an unending bounty, they can relax, knowing they will leave my home feeling full and content. What surprises many of our non-Asian friends is that, as my guests, they will also leave with leftovers to enjoy in the coming days. I stock plastic containers for this very purpose. Family and close friends know they may even bring their own, and I will happily fill them. This does not seem presumptuous in Asian circles. Instead, it signals an intimacy that has been tenderly cultivated over time: *What is mine, is yours. Let me fill your belly to demonstrate how much I love you and then send you home with leftovers so that my love will go with you.*

When Daniel and I were still dating, we went to Boston to visit my Mu Mu (the widow of my dad's oldest brother) and cousins for a post-Christmas gathering. My parents, my brother Greg, and my future sister-in-law were there, too. Three generations of Ngs crowded into the small living room with loaded plates of Mu Mu's home cooking balanced on our knees. The children played on the carpet in front of the TV, which was tuned to a Chinese soap opera with English subtitles for those of us who needed it.

Greg and Daniel were the focus of Mu Mu's attention. Her eyes were alight with satisfaction as they indulged in the steady stream of food she kept piling onto their plates. Strapping young men whose appetites never seemed to be satiated, and for whom my aunt's go-to dishes were novel and far more delectable than their college cafeteria fare. At first, Daniel looked at me with excitement, but as Mu Mu emerged from her kitchen with his fourth helping, even though his third was still in process, his eyes grew wild with desperation. I giggled as I watched the gears turning in his head; he was balancing the screams of his bursting belly with his desire not to offend my aunt in whose home he was a guest for the first time.

Daniel was muscling through his fourth helping like a champ when Greg, always the joker, saw Mu Mu coming out of the kitchen with another dish of steaming chicken and Chinese greens. She went to Greg first, but he held up his hand and said in his most polite voice, "Oh, Mu Mu, that was so delicious, but I can't eat another bite. Daniel, on the other hand, still looks hungry!" While my brother stifled a laugh, Daniel locked eyes with him in a look that said, *Dude, I'm gonna kill you.* I watched with amusement as Mu Mu hurried over to my boyfriend and loaded his plate once again. Daniel managed a smile and a thank you and got back to work. Hours later, as he and I said goodnight, I assured him he had performed well, and Mu Mu clearly approved of him. Why else would she overfeed him in such an extravagant act of love?

In the month of my forty-sixth birthday, a close friend took me to dinner to celebrate, where we talked about our kids, our careers, our aging parents, and our belly fat.

"No matter how much I exercise, it won't go away!" My friend frowned.

"Tell me about it," I bemoaned. "I haven't done anything different, and yet I'm gaining weight."

We shook our heads as we spooned warm apple cobbler into our mouths, surrendering to the realities of perimenopausal existence.

Like many women, I've waged a lifelong battle with my belly. I forcibly lock up its folds behind unforgiving pant buttons and zippers. I suck it in when looking in a mirror sideways. I pull and stretch it back when looking head-on. I give a sour look to its dimples and stretch marks. I curse it as it sags during my morning cat-cows.

My brother and his wife got married during my junior year of college. Heather asked me to be one of her bridesmaids, and I was thrilled to be in a wedding party for the first time. The dress she chose was a beautiful, powder-blue silk *cheongsam* that hugged the body and fell right below the knee. Seeing the sizes available at the store we were instructed to order from, I went for the largest. When the dress arrived at my college mailroom in Ohio, I tried it on and realized with dismay that it needed to be let out. I found a seamstress in the next town over and borrowed a friend's car to get to my appointment. The kind woman there unstitched and restitched the sides of the dress to grant me another inch of breathing room.

Several weeks later, I brought the dress with me to visit my parents for Easter, the wedding now only a couple of months away. My mom had me try the dress on again, but it wouldn't zip up. A talented seamstress herself, my mom studied the seams but looked exasperated.

"There's not a lot of material left to work with," she said. "I can let it out a couple of centimeters more, but that's it. Otherwise, the dress won't stay together."

"Okay, thanks Mom," I murmured, trying not to sound ashamed.

"Just don't gain any more weight before the wedding," my mom muttered, her teeth holding sewing pins as she stuck them, one by one, into the new contours of the blue fabric.

We all say things that others find hurtful, even if it is not our intent. Mothers to daughters especially. It's not that mothers do this more frequently than other people; it's that a mother's words often affect us in ways the words of others do not. Our mother's words carve deep channels in our hearts, and in these channels flow a confluence of beautiful and painful things. All of this is unfair, really, since mothers are usually just trying to show their daughters love. Love, like achieving the near impossible with a needle and some thread.

I'm not sure how Chinese parents are to reconcile what we tell our children when they're young with what we often say to them as they grow older. When they're babies, we pride ourselves on their chubby cheeks and rounded bellies. We tell them *eat, eat!* no matter what they are feeling, because food is considered by Chinese to be the prescription for sadness, joy, and everything in between. We fill their plates and keep an endless stream of extra helpings flowing from the kitchen. We stock the fridge with leftovers and never let them leave the house without something to eat in case they get hungry.

And then, at a moment indiscernible to us and unexpected by them, we start to eye the portions on their plates, tell them they need to eat healthier, and comment—even subtly—on their weight. Somehow, something shifts in the way we attempt to show our children love and concern. Perhaps we begin to realize we can no longer protect them: The world outside of our homes, our kitchens, does not tolerate well the ways we love our children through their bellies. Chinese parents have come to know this. For mothers who are also daughters, we have experienced it firsthand. Perhaps as our own daughters grow, we begin to see ourselves critically, and with less forgiveness. Perhaps we look at them—mirrors of ourselves—and can't help but warn them to suck in their bellies.

On that warm spring day in Missouri, I stood in the lush botanical gardens of the wedding site in my expanded *cheongsam*, with the impressions from two former seams visible as faint lines down both sides of my body. The other bridesmaids at the wedding were smaller-framed than me and I forcefully sucked in my belly, desperate to fit in. I was the only Asian in the bridal party. And in front of God and these witnesses, I wondered how I, a Chinese woman, could feel so ill-fitted in a dress that comes from my own culture.

I wasn't doing well after the birth of my second child, physically or mentally. I had gained fifteen more pounds during my pregnancy than recommended by my doctor and shedding the weight after my daughter was born was not happening as I had hoped it would. My days at home with a newborn, an energetic two-year-old, and an anxious miniature dachshund were long and arduous. Daniel had started his first company, which meant he was working long hours and boarding flights—some of which were international—almost every month. Despite having my parents and a lot of friends nearby, I felt more alone than ever, and when I dared to look at my body below my swollen breasts, I hated what I saw.

In this time, which was likely a season of post-partum depression, I consumed food feverishly and at strange times throughout the day. I snacked when my older daughter snacked. I scarfed down meals in the brief, overlapping minutes that both of my babies went down for their naps. After they went to bed for the night, I ate again while finally enjoying television shows made for adults instead of children. I knew I was binge eating, but I couldn't bring myself to stop.

I remember the first time I put my head into the toilet bowl and vomited up my meal. I struggled with the decision but ultimately decided that what I had eaten was better outside my body than in. My eyes welled with tears as I did it, both from the induced abdominal pressure and from the guilt that wracked my body. Flushing the contents out of sight and out of mind, I cleaned myself up before Daniel got home. I would do this a handful of other times over the next few months until something happened that brought an abrupt end to my dangerous behavior. I had said goodnight to both girls, swaddling my younger in her crib and reading a book to my older daughter, Sage, before tucking her in. I knew I had limited time before Daniel would return from work. After devouring my dinner in a matter of minutes, I went to the bathroom to force it all up. As I leaned over the toilet, Sage suddenly appeared in the doorway.

"Mommy?" she said, sounding frightened. "Are you okay, Mommy?"

I quickly wiped my mouth, clutched my belly, and managed a smile.

"Oh Sagey, yes, I'm fine. I was just feeling a little sick, but I'm all better now."

After washing my hands, I guided my two-year-old daughter back to bed, assuring her of my well-being one more time before kissing her on her forehead.

"Sweet dreams, Sagey," I whispered.

I went into the living room and sat on the couch, my mind wildly awake and racing. A thick fog was clearing as I wept about what my daughter had just witnessed. I thought about how I would feel if either of my girls were to do what I had done. I thought about my belly, burning from its recent trauma, and how it had nourished them both in my womb. I thought about mothers and daughters, light and dark, the opposing energies in us all, and the balancing act required to do right by ourselves and by those we love. I vowed never again to commit such an act of self-violence and to wage more peace than war with my roundest part. I promised to try harder to look upon my belly with compassion and to feed it, nurture it, and offer it some of the generosity I so freely give to others.

HANDS

In the year 1892, U.S. Congress passed the Geary Act—an extension of the decade-old Chinese Exclusion Act that prohibited Chinese laborers from immigrating to the United States. The Geary Act, signed into law by President Benjamin Harrison, mandated that all Chinese persons living in the United States—regardless of birth status—always carry a Certificate of Residence (called a *chak chee* by the Chinese) on their person. At any time, law enforcement had the right to stop any person whom they believed to be Chinese and demand to see their papers. Adding to the humiliation, the required certificate was attainable only with the help of two white witnesses who vouched for the Chinese person's legal status. Possession of a *chak chee* did not grant a Chinese person any new or positive legal rights; instead, it functioned as documentary proof that they were lawfully in the United States. If a Chinese person could not present their Certificate of Residence, they could be charged with a federal crime punishable by a year's imprisonment with hard labor, followed by deportation.

Chinese living in the United States fought back against the new law, protesting through civil disobedience and appealing to those in Washington whom they felt might intervene on their behalf. Qing Ow Yang, the Chinese vice consul in San Francisco, wrote poignantly to his government:

> Do you know what the Geary bill means to the laboring Chinese in this country? It means, sir, that they are placed on the level with your dogs. If you have a dog, a black and tan, a Llewellyn setter, a pointer, you buy a license tag for it and fasten it to the dog's collar, and the number in the dog's tag is its immunity from arrest by the pound-man. Under the Geary bill the laboring Chinese carry their number in their pocket and any man who so desires may stop them and demand to see their "tag". . . . We ask that our government protect its children.[1]

The Certificate of Residence required by the Geary Act was a precursor to the Alien Registration Card that all resident immigrants were forced to carry after the Alien Registration Act of 1940, popularly known as the Smith Act, was signed into law. The former document from 1892 contained information such as the resident's address, occupation, complexion, and "physical marks or peculiarities." The latter document from 1940 included the card carrier's fingerprint.

On November 5, 2024, Donald J. Trump was elected president of the United States for the second time, defeating Vice President Kamala Harris in what most of us had thought would be a tight race. Throughout the evening, news outlets continuously updated the map of the United States, and I sat with my head in my hands, watching the graphic turn redder and redder, county by county, state by state. This was supposed to have been the election that steered the course of our nation away from bigotry and fear, and toward inclusion and hope. Many hands had gone to work to try and make it so. I had signed petitions, donated, and voted in support of the Harris/Walz ticket. Others had knocked on doors, planted banners along streets, and carried signs at rallies. I hand-delivered my older daughter's mail-in ballot while visiting her at college so she could cast her vote for the very first time as a newly turned 18-year-old.

And yet, more than half of our country voted to place Trump at the highest seat of power for a second term. At this writing, the forty-seventh president of the United States is currently carrying out a mass deportation plan that does not distinguish between those he claims to be violent criminals and those without criminal records—families with children and hardworking residents who contribute to their communities. Vulnerable people living in the United States, regardless of citizenship or immigration status, are justifiably frightened as they have been subject to interrogation, search, arrest, and detention by ICE (U.S. Immigration and Customs Enforcement) agents in any place, at any time.

I think about the things that those of us in this country who aren't white are forced to carry at hand: papers, proof, tools for personal protection. But also, the things that are handed to us: anger, distrust, loathing, fragile tears. We hold the weight of having to continually justify our right to livelihood in this country, while the messiness of what is bestowed by those discomfited by our presence overflows, seeping through the cracks between our fingers. We carry generations of these burdens, from our ancestors to our future children. I wonder when and if we will ever be able to lay it all down.

Things that have been handed to me:

- A childhood filled with love and relative safety
- Two kind and wise parents
- A legacy of financial stability
- A body free of disease or disability (thus far)
- The ability to sing in tune
- Meeting my best friend (now husband) so early in life

Other things that have been handed to me:

- Archives of my family history with detailed documentation so I can trace my lineage and tell the stories of my ancestors

- My mother's recipes
- A bundle of bamboo chopsticks salvaged from the Chinese restaurant my grandfather once owned on Beacon Street in Boston
- Boxes of well-loved books that belonged to my parents in college

And still other things:

- My dead hermit crab when I was eight
- Speeding tickets
- Books about Asian eroticism from a white male colleague that led me to file a sexual harassment complaint
- A handwritten letter that broke my heart

Things I want to hand to my children:

- Art: by me, by them, by those we have come to admire
- Traditions that make them feel like they're young again, no matter what their age
- Pieces of jewelry from my mom and her mom
- The best rice cooker on the market as a housewarming gift as each move into their first homes
- Instructions on what to do when their dad and I are gone
- This book, in case they ever want to read it

The only bone I've ever broken was in my left hand. I was in elementary school, and Greg and I were playing a game of footsies on our living room couch. This involved us facing each other with our backs against the armrests, him sitting on one end and me on the other, with the bottoms of our feet pushing hard against each other's until one person's knees would bend and the straight-legged contender was declared the victor. On this day, we were getting rowdy, and his extra three years of leg strength was working in his favor. I was struggling not to let my knees bend, and so I was being lifted out of my seat, higher and higher, until I fell off the back of the couch and onto the hardwood floor. The little bones in my left hand were fractured in a couple of places, and I wore a cast for several weeks.

The only stitches I've ever had were also on my left hand. In seventh grade I stood at the bandsaw in woodshop to make the next cut in what would be a serving bowl—a gift for my parents. The saw hit a knot in the wood, and my pointer finger slid underneath the vertical blade. My middle finger was also nicked in two places. Wrapping my bloody fingers in brown paper towels, my woodshop teacher sent me down to the nurse's office, accompanied by a classmate so I wouldn't pass out in the halls. I needed four stitches that day and wrote an English theme paper later that year titled, "Why Bandsaws Should Be Banned." Pretty handy title if you ask me.

Daniel says my hands are soft, thick, and compact like my mother's. My mom has the same hands as her mother's. Our hands are built for hard work and industry. They are crafted for drafting poems and novels and letters of importance. They're made for art and activism. Our hands are unfussy, thick-skinned, and often dirty. Like my favorite padded gloves from childhood, they can withstand temperatures intolerable to most.

On March 16, 2021, a gunman entered two different spas and a massage parlor in the metropolitan area of Atlanta, Georgia, killing eight people in a horrific shooting spree. Six of the deceased were women of Asian descent. I learned of the tragedy while sitting in my home on a Zoom call with one of my Doctor of Ministry classes. Suddenly, my phone lit up with news notifications and friends texting me to ask if I had seen the news. After gathering the basic details, I apologized to my professor for interrupting and shared what had happened. We were a close-knit group of peers. Eight of the ten students, as well as our professor, are Asian. In early 2021, anti-Asian rhetoric was raging, and acts of hate were all over the news. My professor paused his lesson and together we prayed for rescue and healing.

After class, I sat with Daniel on the edge of our bed and allowed the tears to flow. My body shook with the storm brewing inside of it. A good friend—a Black woman who knows all too well how it feels to be made unsafe in one's skin—texted me to check on my well-being.

"I'm so tired, but I'm also pissed." My hands gripped the phone, my fingers typing furiously.

"I know, sis, I know," she texted back.

"I feel like I need to do something. I can't change everything, but there must be something I can do in my little corner of the world."

A pause. And then three dots appeared on my screen. My friend was typing.

"Today we weep," she said. "Tomorrow, we act."

Within twenty-four hours, I had reached out to several churches, interfaith organizations, and Asian American community groups to invite them to attend an online town hall event. The goal of the gathering was for Asian American Pacific Islanders (AAPI) and allies in our county to discuss possibilities for a community event that would amplify AAPI voices and take a stand against anti-Asian hate in our neighborhoods and beyond. A second but equally important objective was to hold space for AAPIs to speak to our grief and express concerns about what Asians were experiencing all over the world.

At 8:00 p.m. Pacific Time on March 18, two days after the Atlanta shooting, I welcomed more than seventy-five people representing close to two dozen community groups and organizations into my Zoom meeting room. The first thirty minutes were designated as time for AAPIs to speak and for allies to listen. From there, we all brainstormed ideas about what to do next. From this online gathering sprang the organization of a Stop AAPI Hate rally that took place on March 26, 2021. More than 200 people showed up in the San Rafael City Plaza to observe a moment of silence for the victims of the Atlanta tragedy and to listen to speakers who encouraged us to stand together against hate. My oldest daughter, who was fifteen at the time, was among the lineup of speakers.

That online gathering also sparked a task force that worked on getting a resolution passed by our County Board of Supervisors. Resolution No. 2021-16, Resolution of the Board of Supervisors of the County of Marin Condemning and Combating Racism, Xenophobia, and Intolerance Against Asian Americans and Pacific Islanders, was signed on April 13, 2021. I am proud to be one of the co-drafters of the resolution. One of my poems, "The Game Board: Second Generation Chinese American Female Edition," penned just days before the Atlanta shooting, went viral in the weeks following the online meeting. I was given the opportunity to publish and read that poem at several events, and it was also read aloud at protests and rallies from Suffield, Connecticut, to Gainesville, Florida, to Los Angeles, California.

The focus of my doctoral dissertation also shifted because of what I was experiencing at that time. I had been set on the topic of entrepreneurial ministry from when I first matriculated into the program, but when a professor asked us to consider the question, *what keeps you up at night?* I knew I needed to pivot. I began to wonder why there are so few Asian American and Pacific Islander women in ministry called to compensated roles within my denomination, the American Baptist Churches. I set up interviews, downloaded transcripts, and leafed through pages of conversations, seeking insights. I turned through textbooks and biblical commentaries, identifying theological frameworks. I cupped my tired hands around my favorite mug, filled to the brim with steaming *Longjing*, night after night, weekend after weekend. In the end, I published my dissertation, *Voice, Visibility, and Volition: Asian American and Pacific Islander Women in Ministry and the Interrogation of Denominational Systems for Placement and Advancement.*

As a writer, poet, minister, and activist, I commit my hands to the work before me. I commit them to tenderness where tenderness is needed. I commit them to determination where determination is needed. I commit to raising them, clasping them, folding them, and working them to the bone wherever it is needed. Their softness, thickness, fractures, and stitches. I lay all of it down, so that my hands may be of some help.

NOTE

1. Pfaelzer, Jean. "US: China's Example for Today's Latinos." *The Globalist*. August 9, 2019. https://www.theglobalist.com/united-states-latinos-racism-immigration.

LEGS

Origin of the Ng Clan

Ten generations ago, around the mid-1700s, Ng Young was a poor boy. He worked in the fields for a Yee family. Having no home, he built himself a thatched hut next to the road in the rice fields.

One night a Fung Sui (Wind Water) teacher was on his way to Chung Lau. While he traveled, it became very dark, and he couldn't see his way. Soon he realized, that unless he could find some directions, he would be lost. He noticed a light along the road. It was Ng Young's hut. The teacher was welcomed in by Ng Young, and he stayed the night after having dinner.

While they talked, Ng Young told the teacher that his father had died but had no final resting place for his bones since the boy was so poor. In return for Ng Young's hospitality, the teacher said he would travel with him to show him a place for his father. Ng Young's father's name was Ng Leung Sling.

While they were traveling on a side of a hill looking for a resting place, it started to rain heavily. They decided to leave the remains of Ng Young's father against a hill so they could seek shelter. After the rain stopped, they couldn't find the coffin with the remains.

The teacher told Ng Young to cut down the small trees where they had laid his father. They discovered that ants had piled mud all over the coffin until it was completely hidden. The teacher told Ng Young not to move the coffin for it had found its final resting place. When they did open the coffin, they noticed that miraculously the ants had not put any mud on the bones. The coffin rested on the hillside exactly at the "rivet of the scissor." This is what it looks like today.

The final burial of Ng Young's father, Ng Lueng Sling, is the beginning of the Ng village in Hen Slem in Chung Lau. Since that time, the Ng Family has prospered.

My legs were pumping hard. Beads of sweat erupted, then streamed down my temples as I booked it around the trio of holly trees my dad insisted on nurturing in our backyard. The sharp spines of fallen holly leaves pricked the soles of my bare feet, causing me to wince, but I kept going. My porch was just a few yards away. I burst through the screen door, leaving it to swing closed behind me, then pushed into the house and ran up to my room. Slamming the door, I collapsed into the corner by my closet and waited, my heartbeat up to my ears. I knew it was only a matter of time before someone would come for me.

The neighborhood kids had been playing a game of infection tag on our property. Situated on a quarter acre of land, my house featured a wraparound yard with tall pines, a climbable magnolia, hedgerows, and lots of places to run and hide. It was the perfect setting for the fifteen or so kids who had gathered on this sticky July day in southeastern Pennsylvania. My best friend in the neighborhood was Ginny, a brown-haired girl with an athletic build who, at the age of 10, was one year older than me in school. She and I were each other's closest companions during those carefree summer months. Our friendship was boxed in only by the distance our legs could pedal on our bikes before our parents called us in for dinner. We lazed on beach towels on the lawn to tan our prepubescent bodies under the hot sun. We rode our bikes to the office park down the street and raided the vending machine with quarters filched from my mom's purse that hung trustingly by our front door. One morning we started a band that broke up by bedtime that same day. As bandmates, we got so frustrated trying to create the artwork for our cassette tape cover that we decided it was best to consider solo projects.

On that day of neighborhood tag, Ginny and I started off as we always did. We were allies with a strategy: *no matter what, stay together*. But once the whistle blew signifying the start of the game, and kids bigger than us in years and inches started charging, we lost hold of each other. I bolted into the thicket of shrubs that bordered the corner of our property where I crouched in the bed of fallen leaves and branches to make myself invisible. I frantically looked around. No sign of Ginny. I had been waiting for a few moments trying to stay hidden when Marcus, a middle schooler who lived a few houses down from Ginny, bent down beside me.

"I'm not infected," Marcus said.

I breathed a sigh of relief but kept my distance just to be safe.

"Game's changing. Everybody's going after Ginny."

"Ginny? Why?" I asked, peering over the bushes, desperately trying to locate my friend.

"Why not? Plus, she's being annoying."

Marcus stood and ran to the perfect row of hollies just outside my family's sunroom, where we ate dinner every night enclosed under the stars. Other kids had already gathered. I emerged from my hiding spot and approached them cautiously. Conspiratory whispers filled the air. I squeezed between two taller kids, peering into their huddle, and I saw that in everyone's scratched and bloodied hands were piles of jagged holly leaves.

It happened fast but I did nothing to stop it. They pounced on Ginny, and suddenly she was howling in pain as the kids shouted at each other to run before they got caught. Ginny started running herself, in the direction of her own house across the street, her face tear-stained and wincing as she struggled to remove the sharp leaves stuffed inside the back of her shirt. I ran, too. Right around the trio of hollies, into my house, and up to my room.

By early evening my parents had called an emergency neighborhood meeting. All the kids and their parents, including Ginny and her mom and dad, were crammed into our living room. We were scolded and warned. My cheeks flushed with shame. As we went around the room so that each of us kids could say sorry to Ginny, my friend stood rigidly still with her recently washed hair—still wet—clinging to the sides of her face. When it was my turn to apologize, Ginny didn't even look at me.

It wasn't easy being the only Chinese family for miles around, our mere existence an unwitting spectacle whenever we drove into town or went out to eat. We were the only Asian family at our Baptist church in Exton, Pennsylvania, and my brother and I were among only a few Asian students in our school system. On November 23, 1986, our family even appeared on the front page of the *Philadelphia Inquirer*'s Sunday paper. The article was titled "Success Asian-American Style: A small minority fights the stereotypes to gain a prominent presence," and the Inquirer staff writer Mary Jane Fine profiled my mother extensively, writing,

> Although she has vowed not to let her children forget their heritage, she is emphatic that they, and everyone else, know that the family is American. Their annual trip to Center City for the Chinese New Year parade is balanced with can't-miss devotion to the Mummers Parade.
>
> "I vote in every election; I try to be involved, so people can see," she said. "I try to make a difference."
>
> The balancing act seems to be working. Her husband, the Rev. Donald Ng, is on the American Baptist Churches' national staff, where he is involved in youth education. Her daughter, Lauren, 8, and son, Greg, 11, are at the top of their elementary school classes. Upstairs in their split-level home is her skylit studio, artistically cluttered with paint jars, samples and a stack of business cards advertising her new hand-painted furniture venture. Downstairs, the contemporary living room is the stuff of magazine layouts.
>
> "I'm changing stereotypes," she says. "People expect me to use chopsticks all the time. The funny story was, a couple of years ago, my son came home from school and said, 'Mom, can you teach me how to use chopsticks? All the other kids know how.'"

Reading the article again as an adult, I am pleasantly surprised by the gentle resistance it applies to the myth of the model minority even as its characterization of my family keeps it in place. It was 1986 in southeastern Pennsylvania, after all. Dominant Euro-American society was trying to make sense of what it was experiencing via nonwhite immigrant communities and their descendants. We, as Asian Americans, were also trying to make sense of ourselves. The notion of balance is mentioned twice in the newspaper article, as if the identities of *Asian* and *American* are opposites and one must always be striving to find a way to a perceived middle. Unlike the balance of *yin* and *yang* which is harmony found in wholeness.

A photograph of my family in the two-page *Inquirer* spread shows us walking down our street—Crumley Avenue in Malvern, Pennsylvania. From left to right, my dad strides with his hands in his pockets, a toothy smile broadening his face; Greg mimics Dad, hands in pockets, too, and looks to be on the brink of pre-teen self-consciousness; I walk with one hand swinging at my side, the other grasping my mom's, my bowl-cut hair framing my look of curious excitement; my mom appears proud but also wary, as if reserving judgment until the paper is off the presses and she can see for herself how we will ultimately be portrayed. We are walking as if the sheer act of doing so makes the road and the neighborhood ours. We are walking to stake our claim on a place we can call our own. We are walking to belong—in the eyes of everyone who would sit at their kitchen table that November morning with their coffee, orange juice, and bowl of cereal, and open the Sunday paper to look curiously upon our foreign faces.

As a Chinese kid making my way in this milieu of the American 1980s and '90s, typical childhood milestones were run through the filter of my ethnicity. My parents were late to sign Greg and me up for swim lessons, and so, as toddlers swam circles around us at the Malvern Preparatory pool, I could feel the burn of everyone's eyes upon our awkward preadolescent bodies: other parents and swim instructors shaking their heads, wondering why Chinese people don't teach their kids to swim at the proper age. When I was late learning to ride a bike at eight years old and my dad took off the training wheels in an act of tough love, I walked my Huffy Powder Puff Racer to the end of my driveway and straddled its banana seat as the neighborhood kids raced by. When they asked if I was coming, I lied and said I was waiting for a friend. Once they were out of sight, I dismounted and walked my bike back to the garage, kicking out its stand as my shoulders slumped. This didn't feel like a typical childhood failure; it felt like my inability as a Chinese kid to be fully American.

I was desperate to fit in. Fitting in meant being on the inside. Being on the inside meant that someone else had to be on the outside. When Ginny played that undesirable role on that July afternoon of playing tag, my relief that it wasn't me superseded my loyalty to her as a friend. Everyone was pointing at her as the one who didn't belong. She was the object of their disdain. For once, I could simply fade into the background. For once, I was part of the majority.

The story of the *Origin of the Ng Clan* was told to me by my father, who learned it from his mother. It has changed slightly through the years with minor omissions and additions, all seeking to shape an ever more symbolic tale. But exactly what we're expected to learn from this story, I'm not so sure. Certainly, it stresses familial piety; perhaps generations of Ngs are meant to remember how important it is to take care of our ancestors, even in death. It touches on the values of hospitality and the reciprocation of kindness; perhaps we are meant to aspire to the level of generosity our ancestors have demonstrated. It emphasizes duty amid obstacles; perhaps Ngs are encouraged to persevere and weather any storm. It addresses the theme of home and a sense of earthly—and earthy—belonging; perhaps we are meant to remember where we come from, knowing that even if we wander the world as strangers, foreigners, we are indeed rooted somewhere. At the *rivet of the scissor*, the soil is enriched with the bones of our people.

In the summer of 1998, seventeen members of the American Ng family went on a pilgrimage to China. For two weeks, we visited several historical sites and tourist attractions, our bodies stifled in the extreme heat and humidity to which Chinese nationals are somehow accustomed. We walked the barren concrete of Tiananmen Square and wandered the courts and halls of the Forbidden City, rich with dynastic symbolism. We meandered through the lakes and gardens of the Summer Palace and peered into the vast excavation pits lined with terra cotta soldiers in Xian. We climbed ceaseless staircases to temples and pagodas, and cruised down the Li River, Guilin's distinctive karst peaks looming above us like docile giants keeping watch. The culmination of our trip was a visit to our ancestral Ng family home in Chung Lau village, Taishan, which sits in the Pearl River Delta in the southwest region of Guangdong province. We arrived by bus and checked into the only hotel offered in the village. I remember the water in the bathroom sink ran a muddy brown.

The next morning, we made our way deeper into Chung Lau village, to the rows of residences situated between farmed and wild fields. We squeezed through an alley lined with stacked boxes and crates, refuse, and rust-worn bicycles, and then we entered a dilapidated house frozen in time. This was my grandparents' house, and when they last lived there in the 1940s, it was the most modern home in their village. In 1947 my grandmother and uncle pulled the door shut behind them and set sail for America to join my grandfather. He had just returned from Germany, having served as a corporal in the U.S. Army during World War II. The contents of their abandoned house had remained relatively untouched for decades, until my own father visited for the first time in 1982, walking through the structure his father, mother, and older brother had once called home. Gingerly, my dad had picked up bowls, spoons, and decorative vases. He carefully opened closets and drawers to see well-worn clothing and other keepsakes. He sifted through his brother's homework assignments, marveling at the Chinese characters written by hand in perfect form. And on the upper floor, in the last room around the corner from the staircase, he found his mother's bedroom just as she had left it in 1947. He collected some items to bring home with him to Pennsylvania and then closed the door behind him.

Sixteen years later, in 1998, I had the opportunity to visit this family home along with several of my family members. Once we made our way up the crumbling staircase and over to my grandmother's bedroom, we encountered a locked door. Who had locked it, we did not know. And with only a little time to spare and no locksmiths in the village, we were unable to access the room. We left the house wondering what was behind that bedroom door, vowing to get inside the next time we visited China.

My ancestor, Ng Young, left the remains of his father on that hillside because ants had piled mud over the coffin until it was completely hidden. And because the ants had not put any mud on the bones, Ng Young determined that this would be the place for the Ng family to lay down its roots and prosper. Two years before our family pilgrimage to China—in 1996—my Ngin Ngin was admitted to St. Elizabeth's Hospital in Brighton, Massachusetts. She was eighty-four years old, and a cancerous tumor in her breast was causing her other organs to fail. Our family had already begun plans for our pilgrimage, and knowing she wouldn't be there to join us, Ngin Ngin had been busy sharing stories with my father, directing him on who to visit, and drawing maps of where she had hidden jewelry and other valuables throughout the house before she'd set sail for America almost fifty years prior.

When the doctors told us she was dying, my dad drove from Pennsylvania to Massachusetts to sit by his mother's bedside. One day, as she picked at the hospital meal in front of her, my grandmother started shouting and pointing at her tray table. *Ngai ngai! Ngai Ngai!* Ants. She saw ants crawling across the table and tray. They were crisscrossing over her food. Despite my father gently reassuring her they weren't there, Ngin Ngin's face was filled with alarm. She knew our family's origin story, and so, for her, this meant the end was near. It makes me sad to think my grandmother was fearful as she died. Symbolism, for me, always wants to arc toward possibility and hope. Call it a crutch in my grief, but I believe the ants were agents of memory and life, not obsolescence and death. I think the ants were Ngin Ngin's way of seeing our family's imminent return to our home in Chung Lau village.

In 2026, sixteen members of our family will once again travel to China. We'll see the historical sites and get ensnared by the tourist traps. We'll live in that awkward liminal space of belonging neither here nor there—perpetual foreigners wherever we go. We'll marvel at the many ways Chung Lau village has modernized since our last visit almost thirty years ago. The water in the sink will probably run crystal clear. Our legs will take us back to where it all began. Where Ng Young rested during a rainstorm and then laid his father to rest at the *rivet of the scissor*.

I don't expect to feel like I fully belong in Chung Lau village. As modern as it may now be, it isn't home. I never expect to feel like I fully belong in America either, even though I live in the San Francisco Bay Area with its 200,000 Chinese American residents. But belonging, I'm coming to understand, is not just about being part of the majority. It's not about keeping others on the outside so that you can occupy some version of safeness on the inside. Instead, belonging is more about circling back again and again to our origin points. It's about retracing steps and opening locked doors. It's about leaving impressions upon fresh soil that sits atop generations of earth—and stories. It's about the movement rather than the destination and letting our legs—constantly in motion—tell us who we are and who we are becoming.

FEET

Daniel says I have my mom's hands. Mom says I have my father's feet: flat, with no natural arch, prone to dry, cracked heels, but for the most part, reliable. I've never considered my feet to be anything but utilitarian. While I've had a few pedicures in my life, I mostly got myself there for the foot bath, the callus removal, and the massage. The polish always felt a bit ridiculous. After the pedicurist had finished her paintjob, I raised my eyebrows at my dotted digits as if they were detached from the rest of my body. As if they belonged to another woman entirely.

In 2021, my dad and I pointed our feet toward Spain to walk ninety miles of the Camino de Santiago—a spiritual pilgrimage embarked on by hundreds of thousands of people annually and dating to the ninth century when the remains of Saint James the Apostle were said to be first discovered in Northern Spain. Travelers along the Camino, which is also known as the Way of Saint James, are called *peregrinos* (Spanish for pilgrims), and *peregrinos* have several routes from which to choose, each leading to the same destination: the Santiago de Compostela Cathedral in the capital city of the autonomous state of Galicia. My dad and I chose to walk the final stage of the Camino de Portugués, a route beginning in the Galician municipality of Tui, right on the Spain-Portugal border, which would take us through O Porriño, Arcade, Pontevedra, Caldas de Reis, Padrón, and finally to Santiago de Compostela.

Dad and I carried 30L packs equipped with hydration systems and filled with extra layers of clothing, raingear, snacks, medical supplies, and our travel documents. We each had a pair of hiking poles, and we wore shoes that we'd been training in for months. The first couple of days were grand. Clocking between ten-fifteen miles per day across varied terrain, Dad and I marveled at our new surroundings, made jovial attempts to communicate with our fellow *peregrinos* in Spanish, took loads of photos, and talked about all that had come to pass in the forty-two years we had known each other. On the Camino trail markers, characterized by the blue and yellow scallop shell motif and never-failing yellow arrows that pointed the way, we laid small rocks, signifying prayers for those we carried with us on our journey. We wove sticks from fallen branches into a chain link fence, situating them into the shape of a cross, as we gave honor to the One whom we believe always walks with us.

By the third day of our pilgrimage, hot spots started to form on the sides of my toes and the heels of my feet. By day four, those hot spots had turned into blisters, and every step I took was accompanied by searing pain. Every night in our accommodation, I gave myself what I call a "hiker's pedicure." I unwrapped my tender wounds, soaked my feet in warm water, and patted them dry. Then I sterilized a needle and popped each new blister that had formed or reformed, applied antibiotic ointment, and finally rebandaged each foot. This nightly regimen reduced my pain from searing to simply excruciating, enabling me to put one foot in front of the other when we woke the next morning and set off to cover the next several miles.

We walked and we walked. Dad would pause with me when I got to the point that I couldn't walk another step, and I would lean the full weight of my body and gear upon my hiking poles, desperate to alleviate some of the pain. I would breathe deeply, pop a few more Advil, and return to walking. We did this hour after hour, mile after mile. By our final day—a twenty-mile ascent to the cathedral in Santiago de Compostela—the pain was indescribable. My brain had figured out how to detach my feet from the rest of my body so I could process the pain as something outside of myself. I wasn't the one suffering; it was these feeble appendages temporarily attached to my legs that were suffering, and soon enough I'd get to the cathedral, unsnap their clips, and these poor, suffering things would fall from my body to be disposed of forever.

Somehow, by the grace and mercy of God, I made it. Dad and I walked up the steps to the cathedral square, the Romanesque bell towers of that holy sanctuary looming above us like goal posts heralding our victory. I pulled my hiking boots from my throbbing feet, unpeeled my socks from my weeping wounds, and lay right down on the plaza floor, eyes closed, and limbs spread like a fallen angel. Tourists walked delicately around my splayed body. A few people stared. I didn't care, and Dad has the photograph to prove it.

By the time I sat myself up, I had begun to take in the sights and sounds around me.

The atmosphere felt like a party—people taking selfies; a young man playing guitar with his beloved resting her head on his shoulder, singing; families with matching shirts, clearly making the Camino their 2021 family reunion; other *peregrinos* laying on the ground with their backpacks propping up their heads, eyes closed, tired feet unbound from tattered shoes, toes spread and bathing in the sun.

Since our pilgrimage along the Camino de Santiago, I have often wondered what caused my foot injuries that took months to heal. Despite having my father's feet, I suffered immensely while he felt fine. It might have been my choice of shoes; I have since hiked the Grand Canyon Rim-to-Rim trail, choosing trail runners instead of the heavy hiking shoes I wore on the Camino, and I only ended up with two tiny, completely manageable blisters. It might have been my gait, but I haven't done anything to fix that and again, have completed successful long-distance treks since Spain. It might have been my disposition—some sort of intangible thing that couldn't be found in my pack but nevertheless weighed me down enough to alter my posture. Whatever it was, my poor feet bore the brunt of it.

Afong Moy was fourteen years old when she stepped off a trading vessel docked in the New York Harbor and made history as the first recorded Chinese woman to arrive in the United States. It was November 1834, and Moy was accompanied by two U.S.-China traders, brothers Nathaniel and Frederick Carne. The Carne brothers were purveyors of Chinese goods aimed at American consumers, and they hoped that displaying Afong Moy, who was advertised as a "beautiful Chinese lady" with bound feet, would garner attention and gain much-needed sales for their other goods. The brothers procured a New York exhibit space, decorated it like a "Chinese Saloon," and situated Moy in the center of it all as a display. Historian Erika Lee describes the scene:

> Wearing her "national costume," or richly embroidered robes that fit a "lady of her rank," Moy was on display for eight hours a day, from 10:00 A.M. to 2:00 P.M., and then again from 5:00 P.M. to 9:00 P.M. Viewers watched her use chopsticks and listened to her speak in Chinese. An interpreter helped viewers communicate with her, and Afong Moy was instructed to walk around the room to display her bound feet, which were the source of great fascination among men and women alike. The cost for viewing her was 50 cents.[1]

Thus began America's fascination with the Asian woman as object; she is seen as both delicately dainty and exotically grotesque.

My paternal great-grandmother had bound feet. I know this because of the testimony of her daughter, my grandmother, which came to me in the form of 107 pages of typed government transcripts. The story of how those transcripts came to be starts with the Chinese Exclusion Act of 1882. The Chinese Exclusion Act remains the only law in American history to deny immigrant entry or naturalization in the United States based on a specific ethnicity or country of birth. The act was in place when the 1906 San Francisco earthquake caused a huge fire that destroyed public birth documents which led to the proliferation of "paper sons and daughters"—Chinese immigrants who saw an opportunity to work creatively around the racist Chinese Exclusion Act by coming into possession of birth documents not their own. The Chinese Exclusion Act was finally repealed in 1943, but anti-Chinese sentiment and distrust remained high. It was just four years after this Act was repealed, in the spring of 1947, that my Ngin Ngin and uncle arrived on the western shores of the United States on the USAT Admiral Benson, to join my grandfather after he was honorably discharged from the US Army for his service during World War II.

For several months, my three family members participated in hearings arranged by the United States Department of Justice as the Immigration and Naturalization Service attempted to confirm their identities and familial relationship to one another before allowing my grandmother and uncle to reside permanently as citizens. My father obtained the typed transcripts of those hearings from the National Archives many years ago. In them, one sees how my grandfather, grandmother, and uncle were lined up shoulder to shoulder before the interrogation officers, examined like livestock. An officer states that the boy's eyes look like the alleged father's, but there is no facial resemblance to the alleged mother. In another section, one hears my grandfather and grandmother being questioned separately about the number of paces between the front door and the barn door of their village home back in Taishan. The assumption was that if they answered differently, this was evidence of them misrepresenting themselves.

Page 31 of the transcript details verbatim a portion of an interrogation of my grandmother by an immigration officer in which he asks her if her mother's feet had been bound or unbound. My grandmother explains that they were at one point bound, and then later were unbound.

The interrogator asks, "Did your mother have any difficulty walking?"

"Yes, she had some difficulty," replies my grandmother.

The interrogator persists, "How could your mother have worked on the farmland, raising sweet potatoes and other vegetables, if her feet had been unbound?"

And my grandmother answers, "When one must do something, one just has to do it."

Bound feet, also known as "lotus feet," were a mark of feminine beauty that was extraordinarily painful. To achieve this status symbol, a young girl's toes would be forcibly curled under the sole of the foot, thereby breaking the bones in each toe. The arch of the foot was also forcibly broken. Binding cloth was wrapped and tightened around the deformed foot in a repetitive process until the cloth was finally sewn into place. Unbinding would occur regularly to clean and inspect the foot, followed by a fresh rebinding. As painful as it was to have bound feet, it was also excruciating to have them permanently unbound. The deformed shape of the foot could not be reversed. Necrosis, infection, and disease were commonplace. Women with unbound feet were disabled and lived every day with pain that crept up through the rest of their bodies.

And yet, my great-grandmother persevered, toiling in the fields and harvesting vegetables amid the pain of her unbound feet. Perhaps the loosing of bones and flesh liberated other things in her as well: determination, fortitude, beauty standards redefined, practicality over impracticality, and a reconciliation with the earth that cradled her knees in a way it had never cradled her feet, as she bowed in the rich soil, tugging on crisp sweet potato stems that only snapped when she wanted them to.

I had my Ngin Ngin's words, first spoken in Cantonese and then translated into English during the hearing and in the transcript, retranslated into Chinese characters (*hànzì*) by a friend: *when one must do something, one just has to do it*. Those characters are now tattooed on my right arm to memorialize the astounding strength of my grandmother and great-grandmother.

My family loved to go hiking when I was a kid. We set our sights on national and state parks where we could embark on winding, wooded trails and eat our packed lunches beside alpine lakes. We hiked toward volcanic craters and black sand beaches, and toward lighthouses perched on rugged coasts. We laced up our boots to explore rock formations, canyons, and indigenous cliff dwellings. Something about the wide-open welcome offered at these parks drew us in. My parents purchased National Park Passports for Greg and me, and every time we entered a park's visitors center, he and I would proudly produce our pocket-sized, navy-blue books to be stamped with the park's emblem and the exact date of our visit. Then we would purchase the official sticker stamp for that park and carefully affix it to the correct page within one of the nine U.S. regions by which the passport was organized. The park rangers were always friendly with ready smiles and kind eyes. I liked the rangers' uniforms with muted, earthy colors that made them look like they were kin to the trees, trails, and animals they swore to protect. Nodding with their wide-brimmed hats, they would encourage us to have a look around and engage with the interactive exhibits. Sometimes they let us use the rubber stamps to decorate our arms and hands.

Life got busy, as it does, and hiking was not a priority in my young adult years. It wasn't until coronavirus shut down the world in 2020 that I rediscovered my love for the trail. Hiking the open spaces in our neighborhood was the perfect social-distancing activity. Those of us who made the mountains our friends could breathe deeply, in and out, with utmost regard for one another. Safe distances were guaranteed; even on the narrowest of trails, one simply waited patiently for the other to pass by, turning their unmasked face away toward the thicket or sky. My son, who was nine years old when the pandemic began, and our faithful dog, Mochi, set out with me most days to hike and go geocaching for treasures. We enjoyed the extra dose of camaraderie on those trails as we unearthed caches filled with small treasures and added our names to the logbooks. *You were here. We were here. Somehow, we are all here together.*

This is one of the gifts I was given during that strange time: a reminder of how much I long to walk the earth. Our small town in northern California is a highland. It brims with preserved open spaces and boasts small lakes and waterfalls in the rainiest seasons. On my favorite mountain, especially in autumn, sunlight splatters in values of gold across trails studded with towering valley oaks. I love to feel my feet crunching on wintered sprigs and litterfall and to hear the audible stretch of bay branches bending above me, the hammer of acorn woodpeckers hard at work, hollowing out their granary trees. The tawny hillocks rise gently like balls of cream scooped and then sprinkled with a spattering of wildflowers.

I try to get out there every couple of weeks. While I walk every day, nothing compares with being on the open trail. Out there, my soul swells with gratitude for all that has happened to make this possible. All that was sacrificed or given for my feet to be on such a generous path in this very moment. I think about my husband and my kids. I think about my mom, my dad, and my brother. I think about my grandparents, and their parents, and every generation back to the points in history that cradle our origins. I think about my Maker who created an earth with no borders, no in or out, no strangers or aliens. I think about feet that walked the earth in China, Singapore, Massachusetts, New York, Pennsylvania, and California, carrying traces of me in their bones. I think about feet once bound, then unbound. I think about the toil and grief, wonder and joy that come with miles upon miles undertaken so that my sense of belonging somewhere, and becoming the someone I was born to be, can feel hopeful and true.

As I walk, what is it that I carry? I carry the audacity of my hair. The lamplight of my eyes. The conciliation in my ears. The nostalgia in my nose. The blend of bitter and sweet in my mouth. The restful sag of my hospitable belly. The hardiness of my hands. The perpetual motion of my legs. The recognition that I am, as all of us are, born something but always in the act of becoming that very thing.

My feet carry it all.

NOTE

1. Erika Lee, *The Making of Asian America: A History* (New York: Simon & Schuster Paperbacks, 2015), 32.